CONTENTS

CHAPTER 1: Humble Beginnings — 1

CHAPTER 2: The Struggles of Youth — 17

CHAPTER 3: Dreams in the Making — 35

CHAPTER 4: The Big Idea — 49

CHAPTER 5: Built Different — 61

CHAPTER 6: The Money Shift — 69

CHAPTER 7: Collaboration Over Competition — 83

Reflections — 93

About the Author — 107

EVEN ON MY WORST DAY

Because You Never Look Like What You've Been Through

MAURICE WILLIAMS

EVEN ON MY WORST DAY

Because You Never Look Like What You've Been Through

Author: Maurice Williams

Copyright © 2025

All rights reserved. No part of this book may be reproduced or transmitted in any form or by any means, electronic or mechanical, including photocopying, recording, or by an information storage and retrieval system – except by a reviewer who may quote brief passages in a review to be printed in a magazine, newspaper, or on the Web – without permission in writing from the Author.

Edition: Paperback | eBook

Printed and bound in the United States of America.

CHAPTER
01
Humble Beginnings

When people talk about humble beginnings, I know exactly what that means because I lived it.

I grew up in Wheatly Heights, Long Island, New York. Some would call it Wyandanch, a tough but proud community. The first person who comes to mind is my mother. She was a schoolteacher who dedicated her life to educating kids in the Wyandanch School District, an all-Black, lower-income community.

She started teaching Pre-K, then moved on to first grade, fourth grade, and sixth. By the time she retired on June 23, 2006, she was teaching fifth grade. Despite the challenges, she poured everything she had into her students and, more importantly, into raising her four sons. She did it all as a single mother. With the support of my grandparents, James and Dorothy Drayton (rest in peace), she kept our family together, instilling in us the values of love, support, and responsibility. Even on a modest teacher's salary, because let's be real, teachers don't make nearly enough, she provided for us. We didn't always have what we wanted, but we had

HUMBLE BEGINNINGS

what we needed. More than anything, she taught us how to be men, even without a consistent male presence in the household. Our grandfather, James Drayton, was the closest thing we had to a father figure, but it was our mother who carried the real weight. She persevered and never let circumstances dictate our future. I was one of four boys, each with a distinct personality.

My oldest brother, Freddy, loved football and had a reputation you didn't want to test. If I ever got into trouble, all it took was someone realizing I was Freddy's little brother, and they'd back off. He was always in the mix, rolling with a crew, getting into fights, and caught up in the street life. Some might have called him the black sheep, but really, he was just walking his own path. Then there was Derrick. If Freddy was the wild one, Derrick was the glue. Calm, level-headed, and reliable, he had a way of keeping things together. He promoted clubs with his crew, 5-8 Productions, throwing some of the hottest parties on Long Island. Derrick knew how to balance fun with responsibility.

Me? I was the flashy one. I had an eye for the finer things long before I could afford them. I was drawn to the life, the lights, the cars, the yachts, & the beautiful women. At the time, I could only admire them from a distance. I didn't grow up with privilege, but I had vision. I'd cut pictures out of magazines and hang them on my walls as reminders of what I wanted. Looking back, they were affirmations before I even knew what affirmations were. I didn't know how I was going to get it all, but I knew I would. Then there was Randy, the youngest. He was the athlete of the family, also a football player, but more focused on school, sports, and staying out of trouble. He had a solid group of friends and played it safe, at least as far as I knew. That was our household: four very different personalities tied together by one unshakable bond, family.

Growing up, our house sat on the border of two school districts: Wyandanch, the Black district, and Half Hollow Hills, which was predominantly white. Because of the way our home was positioned, I ended up in Half Hollow Hills East. That small twist of fate changed my life. This isn't about disrespecting Black schools; it's about exposure. The resources, the experience, and the opportunities between the two districts were night and day.

At Half Hollow Hills East, I saw things I never knew existed. Kids drove Mercedes and Lexus cars at 16. Their parents were business owners, doctors, and lawyers. They didn't know struggle the way I did. I'll never forget going to my brother Randy's friend Sandeep's birthday party in Dix Hills, Long Island. Sandeep's father was a doctor, and walking into their home was like stepping into another world. Fancy cars in the driveway, perfect landscaping, and inside this massive two-story house with an indoor-outdoor pool. I had never seen anything like it. That moment wasn't about envy; it was about realization. If people were really living like this, then it was possible. It wasn't just something I saw on TV. It was right in front of me.

Another close friend, Aaron, also lived in Dix Hills. We had been best friends since kindergarten, and his family welcomed me like their own. I slept over regularly, eating meals cooked by maids, which was a foreign concept to me. In my house, you ate what moms put on the table. The wild part? Aaron's parents even let him sleep over at my house, despite the fact that we lived in a borderline hood. That mutual trust showed me the stark contrast between the two worlds I straddled. By day, I was around wealth, privilege, and stability. By night, I went home to a neighborhood where survival mode was the norm. That contrast made one thing crystal clear: I couldn't settle for anything less than the life I had seen.

One moment in particular changed the way I viewed everything. We didn't have much growing up. My mother could only afford to buy us clothes once a year in September, that was back-to-school shopping time. That meant throughout the year, outside of that one trip, if my older brother outgrew something, it got passed down to me. I didn't think much of it at first; that was just how things were. But one day at school, I found out how cruel kids could be. I was around twelve or thirteen years old, and my older brother Derrick and I were in school at the same time. One week, he wore a certain outfit: gray sweatpants, tan Timberland boots, and a Champion sweatshirt. A few days later, I wore the same thing, except I tried to switch it up a little, change the shirt, but the boots and sweatpants were the same. I thought I was slick.

But kids notice everything. A girl in class looked at me and said, "Didn't your brother already wear that outfit?"

I felt the heat rush to my face. She wasn't being mean, but her comment hit hard. At that moment, I realized something: I couldn't keep living like this. I was still young, maybe in middle school, but I already knew I had to make a change. Something had to give. I needed money. I needed options. I needed a way to create my own reality, not just take what was handed down to me. That was the day I made a promise to myself. I was going to figure out how to get what I wanted.

In my neighborhood, there were a few corner stores not too far from my house. Near the Long Island Railroad station sat a strip of small businesses: a bodega, a Chinese and Jamaican restaurant, a deli, and a tiny stationery store that sold random knick-knacks. One day, I walked into the stationery store and saw something that caught my eye: fake jewelry. It wasn't much, just gold-plated rings and necklaces, nothing that would fool a real jeweler, but to a kid like me, it was everything.

The best part? It was cheap. A ring might cost five or ten dollars. I didn't have much money, but I scraped together enough to buy one ring. The next day, I wore it to school. People noticed.

"Yo, that's dope. Where'd you get that?"

The reaction was instant. People, especially the white kids, were fascinated. Back then, nobody really knew how to tell the real from the fake. If you had it on, it looked real. That's when my mind started working. If one ring got this much attention, what if I had more? What if I started selling them? They loved the ring so much that I sold the only one I had for about fifty dollars. That same day, I went back to the store and bought twenty-five dollars' worth of the same jewelry. The next day at school, I started selling. But I didn't stick to what I paid. I knew the kids had money, so I raised the prices.

"That ring? Oh, that's exclusive, three hundred."

HUMBLE BEGINNINGS

And the crazy part? They bought it. Just like that, I had a business. I was thirteen years old, walking around school with a pocket full of cash, selling fake jewelry to kids who didn't know the difference. The Black kids in my neighborhood caught on quickly, but the white kids were handing me money left and right. I felt like I had cracked the code.

I had a friend named Steven Joseph. He was half Black, half Puerto Rican, and even though he went to my school, he technically lived in a different district, the Black school district. His parents had used another address to get him into Half Hollow Hills East. One day, Steven and I were walking to the store. He saw me buying the rings. I didn't think much of it at the time. But a few days later, I showed up to school and guess who was selling fake jewelry too? Steven. Not only had he copied what I was doing, but he was undercutting me. Instead of selling rings for three hundred, he was selling them for two hundred. That moment taught me something I would carry for the rest of my life: never tell people your moves before you make them. People will watch what you do, and if they see an opportunity, they'll try to take it. That was the first time I learned the difference between keeping things to myself and sharing too much. Despite the setback with Steven, my hustle didn't stop. I kept selling jewelry, making money, and reinvesting it back into myself. Remember that girl who called me out for wearing my brother's hand-me-downs? That moment stuck with me. It lit a fire in me that never went out.

Between the ages of thirteen and fifteen, I completely changed how I presented myself. This was when brands like Nautica, Polo, and Tommy Hilfiger were big, and I made sure I had them. I took the money I made from selling jewelry and bought myself the kind of clothes I had once only dreamed of wearing. I came to school fly every day. I had a way of mixing and matching pieces that made it look like I had a much bigger wardrobe than I actually did. People started noticing.

"You always fresh, bro."

"I like how you put your fits together."

And just like that, I had gone from the kid wearing secondhand clothes to the one setting trends. That one moment of embarrassment from a classmate changed everything. I made a promise to myself: I would never be in that position again. Looking back, I realize that moment was the seed that would later grow into my own apparel line, Status Plus Fashions. At the time, I didn't know it, but my love for putting together unique outfits, my understanding of fashion, and my refusal to pay top dollar for name brands would all come full circle.

As I navigated my teenage years, I started to realize the importance of learning from people who had already figured things out. That's when I met Shevy Ned. At first, I was closer to his brother, Jason. Jason and I had been friends in school, but over time, I got to know Shevy, and that's when things really changed for me. Shevy was different. He wasn't just another kid from the neighborhood; he was a hustler. While Jason was more laid back, into music, Caribbean vibes, and DJing backyard parties and clubs around Long Island and the city, Shevy was out in the streets moving differently. He was taking trips to Canal Street in Manhattan, buying clothes from the bootleggers, and flipping them for a profit. He was the type of person who could sell anything, from fashion to other things that I won't put in this book.

HUMBLE BEGINNINGS

That energy excited me. He wasn't waiting for money to come to him; he went out and got it. At first, Shevy kept his sources to himself. He wouldn't tell me where he was getting his stuff from. But as we got closer, he started bringing me with him. We would hop on the train to Manhattan, hit up Canal Street, and he would show me the spots where he got the best deals. Watching him, I learned how to move in ways that I had never thought about before. I had already been flipping fake jewelry, but Shevy introduced me to a whole new level of hustling. He taught me how to buy in bulk, how to negotiate with street vendors, and how to build relationships that kept the product flowing. He was the first person I really looked up to in the world of business. He was my mentor before I even knew what a mentor was.

Shevy didn't just hustle; he lived it. That's where I got the term Grind Minister from. I had never met anyone like him before. He wasn't content with just getting by; he was always figuring out the next move. Whether it was flipping clothes, electronics, or something else entirely, Shevy was about his business. And I respected that. For the first time, I wasn't just making money; I was studying someone who had turned hustling into an art form. Shevy unknowingly gave me a blueprint for something that would stay with me for life:

- Always know where to get your product for the lowest price.
- Don't tell everyone your moves; make them first.
- If you're going to sell, sell to the people who are willing to pay the most.
- Reinvest in yourself, always.

These weren't things you learned in school. This was real-world knowledge, straight from the streets, and it shaped how I approached everything from that point forward. There's a big difference between someone putting you on and someone stealing your shine. What Steven did was underhanded. He didn't come to me like, "Yo, teach me how to do this." Instead, he watched, stayed quiet, then popped up selling the same thing at a lower price. What Shevy did was different. Shevy shared his knowledge. He opened doors for me instead of trying to slam them in my face. He didn't move in secret; he moved with me. We worked as a team. That's what separates mentorship from manipulation.

Character matters. People with bad character might get ahead for a moment, but it never lasts. Their lack of integrity will always catch up with them. I've seen it time and time again: folks who took shortcuts, stole ideas, or moved grimy. They always end up stuck, while the people who move with integrity keep leveling up. By the time I was sixteen, Shevy had introduced me to a whole new world of hustling. Then hip-hop fashion exploded. Biggie Smalls, Jay-Z, and Diddy were on the rise, rocking brands like Helly Hansen, Iceberg, Coogi, and Karl Kani. These weren't just clothes; they were status symbols. I had cousins down South in Savannah, Georgia, who loved the styles they saw on TV. But at the time, the South wasn't plugged into fashion like New York was. Trends hit the South late, and access to the latest styles was limited.

When my cousin Shyrone, who lived down South, said, "Man, we love those clothes," a light bulb went off. I took three hundred dollars, went up to Canal Street, and bought as many of those popular brands as I could. I shipped them down to my cousin and told him to start selling them to his crew. This was the start of a whole new hustle selling clothes. A single shirt that cost me forty dollars, I would sell to him for one hundred fifty. And he would flip it down South for three hundred. People down there weren't questioning the price. They just knew these were the clothes they saw on TV, and they wanted in. For a while, it was perfect. Money was coming in, my cousin was making a name for himself, and I was building something solid. But then I learned one of the hardest lessons of my life. Up until that point, I had never been betrayed by family. I had learned lessons about trust from the streets, from business, from so-called friends. But family was supposed to be different.

I sent a big shipment, about fifteen hundred dollars' worth of clothes, to my cousin. He was supposed to sell them and send me my cut. But then he disappeared. I couldn't reach him. I called, no answer. I hit up another cousin, my cousin Man, to find out what was going on. And what did he tell me?

"Oh yeah, Shyrone's around town, selling those clothes you sent."

Selling them. Without paying me back. That's when I realized loyalty isn't guaranteed just because someone shares your blood. So what did I do? I did the only thing I could. I took the loss and re-strategized. I had a choice. I could waste energy being angry and looking for him, or I could pivot and keep moving forward.

I chose to pivot. I learned that trust in business has to be earned, not assumed. It doesn't matter if someone is your friend, cousin, or even your own brother. If they don't move with integrity, you cannot do business with them. That was a painful lesson, but it made me sharper.

I took it as a lesson. At the end of the day, I was still alive. I was still grinding. And I refused to let someone else's lack of integrity stop me from becoming who I was meant to be.

To this day, that cousin has never apologized. No explanation. No remorse. He even follows me on Facebook, but we've never had a conversation about what he did. His mother knew what happened too, but she never said a word. And you know what? That's okay. That's another lesson right there. You have to learn how to win even when you never get an apology. Some people will do you dirty and move on like nothing happened. They might even watch you from a distance, knowing they did wrong but too proud to admit it. If you sit around waiting for people to make things right, you'll stay stuck. I took that loss, kept it moving, and used it as fuel to build something bigger. Because the truth is, people with bad character don't prosper in the long run. They might have a brief shining moment, but it never lasts. Integrity always wins. If I had let betrayal turn me into a distrustful person, I would have missed out on real opportunities. I could have let those experiences make me so guarded that I never trusted anyone again. I could have become one of those people walking around with a chip on their shoulder, refusing to let anyone get close. And if I had done that, I would have missed some of the greatest connections of my life. Case in point: when I met the person helping me write this book, it wasn't because we had a long-standing history. It wasn't planned. We were both at Invest Fest for completely different reasons, doing our own thing. But because I was open to new connections, here we are.

That's what people need to understand. If you let past pain close you off, you'll miss the very opportunities meant for you. You can't let the wrong people block the right ones from entering your life. Looking back, I realize something else. Even though I didn't always love going to church, the values it instilled never left me. My grandfather played the organ; I played the drums. We were in church every Sunday, or almost every Sunday, whether I wanted to be there or not. Even if I wasn't always excited about it, it gave me a foundation. That foundation is why, even after people did me wrong, I never sought revenge. I didn't move grimy, even though plenty of people moved grimy toward me. I didn't let bitterness change my character. At the end of the day, you don't win by stooping to someone else's level; you win by staying true to who you are. And I believe that's why God kept blessing me. Even on my worst day, I refused to compromise my integrity.

Ever since I was young, I was drawn to the light. Not just the spiritual light, but the bright lights, the city life, luxury, beauty. I wanted it all. I wasn't the type to settle for mediocrity. I didn't just want to get by; I wanted to thrive. By the time I was eighteen or nineteen, I had already bought my first luxury car, a 1996 Lexus SC400. Coming from a big city, I was the talk of the town. At twenty, I bought a home in Atlanta, and I was just getting started. Back when I graduated high school, I had no idea what I wanted to do. College wasn't really on my mind, and my mother wasn't the type to let me sit around and figure it out. She gave me two options: get a job or get out. No sugarcoating, no long speeches, just straight-up reality. I didn't have the luxury of waiting for inspiration to hit. We didn't have the internet like today, so I grabbed a newspaper, flipped to the classifieds, and started circling jobs. That's when I came across an ad for a cable puller. At first, I had no idea what a cable puller even was. But the job seemed simple enough. Companies needed their computer systems wired, and a cable puller ran cables through ceilings, floors, and walls.

It wasn't glamorous, but it paid well. For the first time, I was making consistent income without hustling in the streets. It wasn't the final destination, but it was a stepping stone that taught me discipline, responsibility, and the value of multiple income streams. By nineteen, I was making sixty-two dollars an hour working on a special project in Brooklyn wiring their campus. Let that sink in. Most adults weren't making that kind of money, and I was a young man fresh out of my teens. When I pulled up in my Lexus SC400, worth around fifty thousand dollars at the time, people assumed I must be selling drugs. But I wasn't. I was just working, grinding, and investing in myself.

I always cared about my image. Even coming from a tough neighborhood, I never liked the sloppy look. Pants sagging and looking unkempt was never my style. I respected street culture, but I wanted my image elevated. I called it street casual. At seventeen, eighteen, nineteen, I had nice things because I worked for them. People knew me as the well-dressed guy with a clean car who could talk to anyone confidently. I wasn't just a hustler; I was building something. At twenty, I bought my first house. Not rented, not inherited, but custom-built. I took things to another level. This wasn't some random opportunity that fell into my lap. I saw the opportunity and made a strategic move. It all started with my brother Derrick. He was the first in our family to leave New York. At the time, I couldn't understand why. New York was everything to me, the action, the energy, the home I'd always known. Then one day, he asked me if I could drive the rest of his items to Atlanta in his Ford Expedition. I said, "Hell yeah." That trip changed my life.

When I landed in Atlanta, I saw something I had never seen before, Black excellence on full display. Black men and women were thriving, running businesses, driving luxury cars, living in beautiful homes, not just surviving but flourishing. That weekend shook me to my core. I went back to New York with a new mindset: I'm leaving. And by the next summer, I was gone. The timing was perfect. Real estate in Atlanta was affordable compared to New York. I connected with a real estate agent, and before I knew it, I was having a house custom built for one hundred fifty thousand dollars. I wasn't renting; I was creating a foundation for my future. The crazy part was that for almost two years, I still lived in New York even though my house was finished. I would fly down on the weekends, stay in my house, then fly back to New York to work. At nineteen and twenty, I had already positioned myself ahead of most people my age.

I tried to put my people on, telling my homies, "Yo, we gotta get out of New York. The promised land isn't here." But they weren't ready. They believed New York was everything. They didn't know anything else, and they weren't willing to take the risk. But I had seen what was possible, and I was determined to build a life beyond what I had known. People always ask why I never went to college. The answer is was simple at the time I thought: I didn't need it. I had been making money since elementary school and built multiple streams of income before I could legally drink. Why take on debt for a degree when I was already making more than most college grads?

At nineteen, I was making sixty-two dollars an hour. I even told girls with college-educated parents, "I make more money than your daddy." And I wasn't lying. College is valuable for the right people, but for me, my path was entrepreneurial. Hustling, networking, and strategy would take me further than any classroom. There's a difference between making money and building wealth. Most people go to college to get a job and make money. I already knew how to make money without a job. The next step wasn't just about income; it was about ownership. That's why I invested in real estate at such a young age. I was thinking about the next ten years, not just the next paycheck. That mindset set me apart. By the time I settled into Atlanta, I knew one thing: this was just the beginning. I had made it out of New York, built my first house, and proven that hustle, strategy, and vision could take me places most people never imagined. But I wasn't done yet. Because once I got to Atlanta, everything changed again.

CHAPTER
02
The Struggles of Youth

In life, failure is unavoidable. Some moments sting only briefly, like a small embarrassment you can laugh about later. Others hit much harder, missed opportunities that feel like a punch in the gut that can change the entire course of your life. But here is the truth I have discovered: failure is not the end, it is the seed of growth. Looking back, I can trace my journey to three defining failures. At the time, each one felt like a crushing setback, the kind of moment that makes you question yourself. Yet those same experiences became the foundation of my resilience, teaching me lessons I carry to this day.

Lesson #1: Preparation is Everything

I was young, maybe in my late teens, when I ran with a crew in New York. We called ourselves Arch Angels, a tight circle of Caribbean kids from Trinidad, Grenada, and Jamaica. Our world revolved around music and entertainment. We rapped, DJ'd, and hyped the crowd on the mic the way it is done in Caribbean culture, lively, raw, and full of energy. I wasn't Caribbean myself, but you couldn't tell from the way I carried myself. Being around them, soaking in their culture, their rhythm, and their confidence, it was as if I had been born into it. For me, it wasn't just hanging out; it was an education, and those moments shaped how I approached performance and creativity.

One day, we got a huge opportunity, a chance to audition for a mixtape feature. For us, this was everything. The thought of stepping into a real New York studio and putting our music out into the world had us hyped. We just knew we were ready.

But the truth? We weren't.

We had bars. We had energy. But we had never actually rehearsed together. So when it came time to perform, it was chaos. We weren't coordinated. We didn't understand the rhythm of moving as a group. We jumped in at the wrong times, cut each other off, and bounced around without any structure. The producers looked at us like clowns.

That day, I learned a hard lesson: opportunities don't mean anything if you're not prepared to seize them. I carried that lesson with me into everything I did afterward, whether it was business, networking, or eventually launching Status Plus. Looking back, I know that if we had shown up to that audition prepared, if we had rehearsed, structured our performance, and walked in like professionals, we might have had a real shot. Instead, we walked in like amateurs and walked out like nobodies.

That is why, to this day, I don't take preparation lightly. It's not just about showing up, it's about showing up ready.

Lesson #2: If You're Not Ready, You'll Fumble the Bag

Failure doesn't just happen on stage. It happens in business and career too.

I remember one time when I was looking for a new job in IT. My cabling skills had leveled up since my first introduction to computers, and I finally felt ready for the next step. Then came the call. It was a big interview in Manhattan, in a huge skyscraper overlooking the water. Just walking into that building felt like money. The opportunity was huge, and I knew it could change everything for me.

Coming from the streets, from hustling the way I did, and with all that I had accomplished at a young age, I thought I could take on the world and anything in it. Boy, was I wrong. This was a different monster, one I wasn't prepared for.

When I sat down for the interview, I bombed.

Every question they asked, I either answered wrong, stumbled through, or couldn't answer at all. Instead of holding my composure, I kept admitting I was nervous, as if that would somehow help my case. It didn't.

Looking back, I know exactly why I failed:

1. I wasn't prepared. I hadn't researched the company or practiced common interview questions. I walked in blind, thinking I could wing it.
2. I let my nerves control me. Instead of projecting confidence, I showed them doubt.
3. I assumed they were smarter than me.

That last one was a big misconception I carried when I was young. I used to believe that people in power — business owners, CEOs, managers — must automatically be smarter, sharper, and more capable than me. I even thought grown-ups, older people, and even parents, including mine, had life all figured out. I thought they were wise and had the answers. But in reality, many of them were just like me, if not worse, still trying to figure things out as they went.

The truth is, most people are just winging it.

The difference is, they move with confidence. Even when they don't have all the answers, they own the room. If I had walked into that interview with confidence, even without perfect answers, I probably could have turned things around. But instead, I let my lack of preparation and self-belief cost me a huge opportunity. Now, when I walk into a room, I own it. I understand that confidence plus preparation equals success. And that's something I carry into Status Plus, teaching others that if you don't prepare and believe in yourself, you'll fumble the bag every time.

Lesson #3: Family Can Let You Down, But You Have to Keep Going

The third lesson was one of the hardest ones to swallow. When I was younger, I truly believed that family had your back no matter what. I thought blood meant loyalty, that no matter what happened in life, family would ride for me the way I rode for them.

But life showed me otherwise.

EVEN ON MY WORST DAY

I had built a business shipping high-end clothes from New York down South, where demand was high. My cousin, someone I trusted, someone I broke bread with, was supposed to be my business partner. His role was simple: sell the clothes and send me my cut. One day, I sent him a fifteen-hundred-dollar shipment worth fifty thousand once sold, but instead of handling business like we agreed, he disappeared. No call. No explanation. No apology.

Even worse, his own mother knew what he did, and she stayed quiet. That betrayal cut deep. It shattered my belief that family always does right by you.

Coming from the streets, I was used to watching my back with strangers. But I never thought I'd have to guard myself against my own blood. To this day, my cousin has never acknowledged what he did.

But you know what? I didn't let it stop me.

I could have folded. I could have sat around angry, waiting for an apology that was never going to come. Instead, I took the loss, swallowed the pain, and kept moving. That fifteen-hundred-dollar loss became a fifty-thousand-dollar lesson in disguise: trust has to be earned, even with family.

And that mindset changed the way I do business forever.

Because here's the truth: you can't let other people's bad character ruin your future. Each of these moments - the failed audition, the botched job interview, and the betrayal by family- felt like losses at the time. But now, I'm grateful for them. The audition taught me that preparation is key. You can have talent, but if you're not organized, you'll lose opportunities. The interview taught me that confidence can make or break you, and that most people aren't as put together as they seem. The family betrayal taught me that trust in business must be earned, not handed out just because someone shares your blood.

Looking back, I wouldn't change a thing. Because those failures weren't dead ends; they were seeds. Seeds that grew into wisdom, resilience, and the drive that makes me who I am today. And that's exactly what Status Plus Fashions is built on. My brand isn't just about clothes; it's about lessons, growth, and the belief that "even on your worst day, your status is plus". Every design, every message, carries the reminder that pain can be turned into power, and losses can be flipped into lessons.

Lesson #4: Just Because Someone Looks Successful Doesn't Mean You Can Trust Them

I knew Kelvin through my high school friend Gomal. Gomal and I went to different schools. I went to Half Hollow Hills East and Gomal went to Half Hollow Hills West. Same district but different schools. We'd see each other in passing because we both played sports, and sometimes our schools would face off as rivals. After graduation, Gomal moved down to Atlanta. That's where we reconnected, and through him, I got closer to Kelvin, his first cousin. Coming from Wheatley Heights/Wyandanch, we were supposed to be family. We hung out a lot, shared the same roots, and grew up with the idea that family had your back.

Real estate was booming in Atlanta, and Kelvin had already built a company. When he suggested a joint investment, I trusted him.

The plan sounded solid:
We'd buy a house using my credit.
Pull about thirty thousand dollars in equity.
Split the cash fifty-fifty, fifteen thousand each.
Fix up the house and rent it out for passive income.
Continue building the business together.

I was only twenty years old. I didn't know the ins and outs of real estate, but I assumed he'd take the lead since he had experience. At first, everything went smoothly. We closed on the house, pulled the equity, and I got my fifteen thousand. I was assuming Kelvin was handling the property like we agreed. But Kelvin had no intention of reinvesting in the house. He used his share for himself and disappeared. Months later, the mortgage came due. The house wasn't rented out. No income. No plan. And no Kelvin. The property went into foreclosure, and my credit, something I had worked so hard to build, was damaged.

The financial hit stung, but the betrayal hurt even more. He played the friendship and family card to get what he wanted, knowing all along he wasn't going to follow through. That experience taught me one of the hardest lessons in business: just because someone looks successful doesn't mean they have integrity. Kelvin dressed the part. Talked the part. But behind the curtain, it was smoke and mirrors. Now I don't play those games.

I don't care if you're my friend, cousin, or even my brother. If we do business together, there's going to be a contract, a strategy, and accountability. Trust without accountability is a setup for failure.

That lesson became a pillar in how I move today, not just in real estate but in Status Plus Fashions. Every design, every collaboration, and every business decision carries that same principle: integrity matters more than appearances. Even when the world seems flashy, even when others try to take shortcuts, we focus on building real value, honesty, and trust. That's why Status Plus isn't just a brand; it's a reflection of resilience, authenticity, and the belief that even on your worst day, your Status is Plus.

Lesson #5: Even Your Closest Friends Can Betray You

I had another best friend in Atlanta. His name was Q. Me and Q ran the streets like Big and Puff. We were tight. He always knew how to move in the city, buying and selling, making deals, and staying connected. At one point, I was looking for a new ride. I had found a car that I almost could not live without. It was a BMW 645 Convertible CI, a top-tier luxury car with twenty-two-inch rims. I talked to Q, and he promised to make the deal happen. Q had a car dealer's license and connections that could get luxury cars and bank financing while bypassing the usual red tape. At the time, I thought that red tape was impossible to navigate on my own, so I trusted him to handle the deal. What I didn't realize was that if I had taken the time to understand the process, I could have done it myself.

The car didn't come from a dealership. It was from a private seller. I assumed the process would be completely different, and it was, but not by much. Had I just explored financing and taken a loan myself, I would have saved money, time, headache, and pain, and I would have come out way better.

I trusted Q, gave him fifteen thousand dollars in cash, and traded in my current car, a paid-off 2005 Mercedes-Benz CLK 320, as part of the deal. At first, everything seemed legit. But when it came time for delivery, he kept making excuses.

"Oh, there's a delay, bro."
"They had to do some extra work on it."
"I'll have it for you next week."

Weeks went by. Then one day, I found out the truth. He was joyriding in my car. My car, the one I had paid for. That moment broke me. Not because of the money. Not even because of the car. But because this was someone I trusted like a brother. After everything we'd been through, he still chose greed over loyalty. I had to face a harsh reality: even the people closest to you can betray you.

After that, me and Q were done. The friendship was ruined. The trust was gone forever.

These experiences forced me to rethink business, money, and trust. The failed real estate deal taught me that experience doesn't always equal good intentions. Q's betrayal showed me that even those closest to you can put greed first. And the foreclosure taught me the importance of financial responsibility and staying fully involved in my investments. Even though these situations hurt, they didn't break me. They made me wiser, sharper, and more strategic. Because one thing about me: I might take a loss, but I never stay down.

Betrayal, heartbreak, and loss either break a man or build him. For me, every time someone tried to break me, I came back stronger. But that doesn't mean the pain didn't leave scars. Each moment of failure was a lesson, not just in business but in character, self-worth, and resilience. This last moment of failure was different. It wasn't about money; it was about the heart. And it taught me that trust is sacred, loyalty is priceless, and no one, not even a brother, gets a free pass.

That lesson is part of why Status Plus Fashions exists. Every design and every message reflects the reality that even on your worst day, after betrayal, setbacks, and heartbreak, your Status is Plus. It's about resilience, strength, and knowing that what tries to break you can actually make you.

Lesson #6: Some People Will Never See Your Worth No Matter What You Give Them

I had been dating a girl in Atlanta. Her name was Tamekia, and she was from Orangeburg, South Carolina. We were together for about three or four years. It wasn't perfect. We had arguments, disagreements, and tension, but I loved her. I thought we were building something.

This was the first time I ever dated a girl from the South. Growing up in New York, I knew how girls from the city could be rough, but I thought Southern girls were sweeter. Boy, was I wrong. Some Southern girls are just as grimy. Coming from the New York streets, I didn't fully know the Southern streets. They were a little different, but in a lot of ways, the same.

EVEN ON MY WORST DAY

At the time, they called me Diggs. They still do if you know me from the old days. This was my first real Southern love, and I was knee-deep. It took a lot to convince me that she wasn't the person for me. I knew she loved me, but she had never known a love like this before, and when she met me, she didn't know how to handle it. Her past unhealthy relationships and trauma made things complicated.

Coming from a strong, structured household in New York with close-knit community relationships, I assumed everyone had that same foundation. Tamekia didn't. Coming from a broken home, she didn't have the best upbringing. I later found out she carried a lot of trauma that she had never dealt with. At the time, I didn't even know people could grow up with so much unresolved pain.

When I first got with Tamekia, it was all good. She came off sweet, loving, and caring, the type you think you can build with. But once we got closer, I started seeing the other side of her - the dark side. Violent & Toxic. One thing I learned is that when people get too comfortable, they either start taking your kindness for weakness, or you finally see who they really are. With her, I saw both. We moved in together and stayed like that for about a year. She never worked a day, but I had a steady job, so I covered everything—the rent, the bills, the food. I could hold down the basics, but not her extras. That's when the fights started. And they weren't just arguments. They got physical. To the point where the cops were called. More than once.

Eventually, I had enough. We broke up, and she moved out. But before all that, I noticed something was off. She started popping up with

THE STRUGGLES OF YOUTH

money. But I knew damn well she didn't have a job. When I asked about the money and where it came from, she hit me with, "I got a part-time gig." I knew that was a lie. I just didn't know the truth yet.

The way I found out what she was doing was through my best friend Shawn. We were roommates, and he had noticed her behavior was way out of the norm. Shawn was from Macon, Georgia. He knew the world she came from, a world I had no idea even existed. One day he pulled me aside and said, "Yo Diggs, I know you love this girl, but she ain't right. There are some things I have to show you."

Craigslist was big back then, and they had a dating section where people could hook up. Shawn told me to give him her number, which I did. Then he put it into Google, and sure enough, a few profiles popped up with her name. There were even ads posted showing how to contact her for "a good time."

I couldn't believe it. Right there, in front of my eyes, she was on the internet selling something sacred that was supposed to be mine. I thought I wasn't doing enough, but Shawn assured me I was. The truth was, she had a dark spirit and a rough upbringing, and she had never been used to a good man like me. That moment shattered me. I realized that some people will never see your worth no matter what you give them. It wasn't about what I didn't do. It was about her own brokenness, her choices, and her inability to value what was good in her life.

I forgave her, not for her, but for me. Because at the end of the day, I knew I had to love myself more than I loved her. That's the only way to keep moving forward—by recognizing that other people's brokenness is not a reflection of your own worth.

That lesson stuck with me. In life, in business, and in relationships, some people simply won't recognize what you bring to the table. And that's okay. What matters is how you hold yourself, how you keep moving, and how you protect your value.

Lesson #7: Karma Always Comes Back So Stay True to Yourself

The funny thing about life is that what goes around always comes around.

The same people who did me wrong—God dealt with them. The friend who scammed me in the car deal? He turned into an alcoholic. The one who robbed me in real estate? Lost everything. I never had to lift a finger. I never had to seek revenge.

Because I knew God was handling it. And that's what people don't understand. You don't have to stoop down to their level. You don't have to try to make things even.

When you walk in the light and have good intentions, it will show. Maybe not now, but later it will, I promise you this. When you live with integrity and keep moving forward despite what people do to you, life has a way of handling the rest. What they stole from me? I got back tenfold. What they tried to take? God replaced with something greater.

As far as my ex Tamekia, to this day she tries to reach out to me. Even after all her failed relationships, I guess when you get older and mature, you realize the mistakes you make, but sometimes it's too late to fix them. As for my cousin, he still lives in Savannah, Georgia. From what

I've been hearing, his mother has been sick and he hasn't been doing too well. I wish them all the best.

But here's the lesson: when you do people dirty intentionally, it will come back to you.

That's why I keep moving the way I do. I refuse to let their actions define me. I refuse to become cold, bitter, or angry because of their choices. Because at the end of the day, I refuse to be where they are now.

Lesson #8: When You Have a Moral Threshold You'll Always Rise Above

I've been through a lot, and I could've easily gone down the wrong path. I could've become the scammer, the schemer, the man who takes advantage of others before they take advantage of me. But I didn't. Not because I was perfect. Not because I didn't have temptations. I may not have been the best version of myself or the perfect church boy all the time, but I was raised in the church. And no matter how far I went, something inside me always knew when to stop.

There were lines I wouldn't cross, no matter how much money was on the table. There were choices I refused to make, even when the world made it seem normal. Because when you have moral boundaries, you don't fall into the traps that destroy other men. You don't get caught up in the things that end in regret, pain, and downfall.

And that's why, even through everything I've been through, I can say with confidence: I still don't look like what I've been through. This is why I live, breathe, and scream my slogan:

Even on my worst day, my Status is Plus.

Some things in life just don't make sense to me. I understand hustling. I understand struggle. I understand doing what you have to do to survive. But what I will never understand is people who have no regard for others. I've seen people lie, cheat, and steal, and I've had people betray me in ways I never saw coming. And every time, I found myself asking the same question:

"Don't they feel anything? Doesn't their soul tell them this is wrong?"

It's one thing to grow up without a strong moral foundation, without guidance, without parents teaching right from wrong. But even without that, isn't there something in your spirit that tells you when you're crossing a line? Isn't there some internal warning that says, "Hey, this is not okay"?

Because for me, even when I was younger and wilding out, there was always a threshold I wouldn't cross. I wasn't perfect. I made mistakes. But something in me always knew my limits. And I think that's what separates people who evolve and grow from people who keep repeating the same destructive cycles. Some people are addicted to drugs. They will sacrifice their families, their health, and their futures just to chase the next high.

But some people are addicted to success, to greed, to power. And just like a drug addict, they will do anything to get it.

They don't care who they hurt.
They don't care what they have to sacrifice.
They don't care how much destruction they leave behind.

To them, nothing else matters except winning. And that's dangerous. That's why I had to cut certain people off, because I realized some people don't have any moral boundaries. If you don't prioritize integrity, family, and respect, you'll do anything. And I refuse to be around people who live like that.

If I had to summarize everything I've learned in this phase of my life, it would be this:

1. Not everyone has the same morals as you. Don't expect them to.
2. Some people will betray you, and you have to keep moving forward anyway.
3. Success and greed can become addictions so stay grounded.
4. Playing the long game will always beat cutting corners.
5. You don't have to seek revenge; life will handle it for you.
6. Have a moral threshold. Know your limits. And never let anyone pull you past them.

Because at the end of the day, I don't care how much money you have or how much success you think you've gained. If you had to lie, cheat, or steal to get it, you already lost. As for me, I'll take the long road. Because when I win, I want to win with clean hands and a clear conscience. The only kind of success that matters is the kind you can sleep peacefully with at night.

Even on your worst day isn't just words on a shirt. It's a reminder of resilience, integrity, and self-respect. It's about showing up even when life knocks you down. It's about facing betrayal, failure, and loss without letting it define you. Even on your worst day, you can rise, maintain your dignity, and keep moving forward. That's the true meaning of Status Plus.

CHAPTER

03

Dreams in the Making

The spark of entrepreneurship can ignite in anyone, at any stage of their life. But for young people—especially those who've never seen entrepreneurship up close—it can feel distant, almost untouchable. The question becomes: *How do you discover that spark? How do you know if it's your path to pursue?*

For me, it started with **curiosity**. I didn't grow up around CEOs, investors, or people running companies. What I did grow up around was hustle—the kind of hustle you see every day in the streets and in people just trying to make ends meet. That was my first introduction to entrepreneurship, even though at the time I didn't know to call it that. I was just watching people find ways to survive.

But survival isn't the same as vision. My curiosity pushed me to look deeper. I started asking questions, observing, and wondering what else was out there beyond my immediate surroundings. I didn't just want to see someone else's hustle—I wanted to understand how to build something of my own.

DREAMS IN THE MAKING

There's a saying: *"Curiosity killed the cat."* But in entrepreneurship, curiosity gives you life. It fuels growth, discovery, and the courage to try. And the more curious I became, the more I realized the world was bigger than the block I grew up on.

That's why I say: don't let your environment put limits on your imagination. Your surroundings may shape your perspective, but they don't define your possibilities. When you allow yourself to dream beyond the familiar, you begin to see new paths, new opportunities, and new ways of living. And that's exactly where entrepreneurship is born.

But there's something important to keep in mind—life often works like a game of telephone. What you hear isn't always the truth. That's why it's crucial to do your own research and go straight to the source. Don't just take things at face value, especially when it comes to advice about your future. People may try to guide you, but you have to be intentional about how you listen and selective about whom you listen to.

Often, it's not people's words but their actions—the way they move, talk, and carry themselves—that reveal the most. And for someone growing up in an environment where asking questions could be seen as disrespectful, this lesson becomes even more valuable. I didn't face much resistance personally, but I know it's common for young people to be discouraged from being too curious.

Still, I've always believed in the power of asking—when it's done with respect. Curiosity without respect can come off reckless, but curiosity with respect turns into wisdom. When you strike that balance, you gain the ability to learn from others' experiences instead of repeating their mistakes.

Being curious was the foundation of my growth, but much of my drive came from watching my mother. She worked tirelessly to provide for us, even when the odds were stacked against her. No matter how tough things got, she never gave up. Seeing her resilience made me realize that if I wanted more for my life, I couldn't keep depending on anyone else to make it happen. I had to take ownership of my future, just like she took ownership of our survival.

From her example, I learned that hard work means nothing without action. Momentum became my biggest lesson. I saw how quickly life could change, how opportunities could come and go, and I understood that if I hesitated too long, I might lose my chance. Watching my mother move with urgency to keep us afloat taught me the same principle: when something matters, you act on it. For me, the key to success was to execute fast, before doubt or distraction could get in the way.

When it comes to overcoming doubt, I can honestly say I never allowed it to stop me. Instead, I leaned on a deep sense of purpose and belief in what I was building. Once you've been through real struggles and seen how difficult life can get, you develop a confidence that says, *If I made it through that, I can make it through this.*

That mindset fueled everything I did with Status Plus. I built my work ethic around it. No matter how tough things got—whether it meant working long hours, walking miles just to catch a train, or crashing on couches when I had no place to stay—I refused to let doubt control me.

For me, belief wasn't optional; it was the foundation that kept me moving forward when everything else told me to stop.

In those moments, doubt wasn't even a consideration. I was willing to put in the work, no matter the circumstances. That's what makes a true entrepreneur: the ability to keep going, even when it feels like everything is falling apart.

I had lost everything once before. I spent a short period in jail, and when I came back, everything I had worked for was gone. The people I trusted had taken it all—my belongings, my finances, everything I had built. But even in that situation, I didn't let doubt consume me. I knew my worth, and I knew I could rebuild from the ground up.

It all comes down to character and integrity. When you cultivate strong relationships based on trust, you can always call on people for support. And even when everything seems to crumble, your hustle, resilience, and belief in yourself will carry you through.

That's the essence of Status Plus: *Even on your worst day, your Status is Plus.* It's a mindset. It's knowing that no matter how much you've lost, how many setbacks you face, or how difficult the path gets, your value, your drive, and your ability to rise above remain intact. Every challenge becomes fuel, every setback a lesson, and every day an opportunity to prove to yourself that you're unstoppable.

I didn't feel sorry for myself. I didn't let the setback define me. If I had it once, I knew I could get it again—bigger and better. That's the essence of entrepreneurship: taking setbacks, turning them into lessons, and using them as stepping stones to build something greater.

When people tell you to play it safe, they don't understand the drive that comes with being an entrepreneur. They don't see the bigger picture, and they certainly don't understand the sacrifices required to create something valuable. Playing it safe is for those who fear risk—but real growth comes from embracing risk and facing challenges head-on.

Don't let fear of failure stop you. The risk is part of the journey. You have to believe in yourself and your vision, and when you do, the rewards far outweigh anything a "safe" choice could ever offer.

If I can do it, you can do it. If I got it once, I can get it again—bigger and better. I've always believed that success isn't about playing it safe. When you get caught up in the idea of "safe," you miss opportunities to stretch yourself and break free from the limitations society often tries to impose.

Growing up, I wasn't taught to play it safe—I wasn't taught to take the easy route—and I'm grateful for that. It's the risks, the sacrifices, and the tough decisions that have brought me to where I am today.

The mentality of "play it safe" is everywhere. It's in the advice people give: *"Go to school, get that government job, work your nine-to-five, and save for retirement."* People hear it so often they start believing it's the only way to live. But let me tell you—taking the "safe" route doesn't lead to extraordinary outcomes. It doesn't lead to the freedom you want, the lifestyle you dream of, or the impact you're capable of making on the world.

That's why *Status Plus* isn't just a brand—it's a mindset. *Even on your worst day, your Status is Plus reminds* you that no matter what setbacks or risks you face, your value, your drive, and your ability to rise above define your story. Playing it safe might keep you comfortable, but stepping up, taking risks, and trusting yourself is what builds greatness.

I look around at people who've played it safe their whole lives. They work their jobs, pay their bills, and follow the same routine year after year. They never take vacations, rarely enjoy life, and never seem to get ahead. And you know what? Playing it safe hasn't given them the life they dreamed of.

For me, I wanted more. I wanted the things I saw on my vision board—the cars, the houses, the experiences, the lifestyle that comes with freedom and success. Playing it safe wasn't going to get me there. The "safe" route often leads to mediocrity, and I wasn't willing to accept that.

To me, playing it safe was a recipe for stagnation. It was the "get by" mentality, the "good enough" mindset. But good enough was never enough for me. I didn't want to settle for small raises every few years or struggle to make ends meet on a paycheck that barely covered my needs. That wasn't the life I was willing to live.

Instead, I took risks. Every decision, every opportunity, every moment I had to make a choice—it came down to whether I was willing to take the leap and bet on myself. And most of the time, that leap came with uncertainty, discomfort, and the fear of failure. But guess what? It was worth it. The risks paid off.

The people who play it safe, who say you shouldn't pour too much into your dreams, don't understand what it truly takes to build something great. They don't get that sometimes you have to take bold risks to see real rewards. You have to be willing to invest in yourself, your brand, and your future.

Playing it safe might help you avoid failure—but it also keeps you from achieving success. I wasn't willing to let fear control me. I wasn't afraid to invest my time, money, and energy into creating something bigger than what I had. I wasn't afraid of failing, because failure wasn't the end—it was just another lesson on my path to success. And you know what? I don't regret it. If I had played it safe, I wouldn't be anywhere close to what I've accomplished today.

Some people may tell you not to go all in, not to risk it all. They may tell you to save for a rainy day, but here's the truth: when you have the drive, the vision, and the will to succeed, your "rainy day" becomes your motivation—not your excuse. You can always find a way to bounce back. If you lose everything, you can rebuild. And you'll rebuild stronger.

That's the difference between those who play it safe and those who take the leap. It's not about avoiding failure; it's about learning how to use failure to your advantage. In the end, it's not the person who avoids the storm that grows—it's the one who faces it head-on and comes out stronger.

So don't be afraid to take risks. Don't be afraid to invest in yourself. Don't play it safe. The path to greatness is never easy, and the rewards aren't handed to you on a silver platter. But if you're willing to bet on yourself and take those risks, you'll achieve more than you ever thought possible.

Not playing it safe has, without a doubt, been one of the greatest blessings of my life. When you step outside your comfort zone and take that leap into the unknown, you open yourself to possibilities you never imagined. It's in those moments of uncertainty that you discover your true power, your abilities, and your potential.

You realize just how much you're capable of when you stop holding back. If I had played it safe, I would never have uncovered the depth of my own potential or the doors that were waiting to be opened. One of the greatest gifts of taking risks is discovering just how resourceful and capable you are when faced with adversity. You never truly know what you can accomplish until you push yourself to do the things that scare you.

In 2015, I was working a tech job in Miami for a company called Telx, which was later acquired by Digital Realty. When the purchase was completed, they laid me off. I said to myself, "This is not me. I'm tired of working for someone else." I had a little bit of savings, so I thought, why not try to start my own IT consulting company? I was professional, had strong networking skills, plenty of contacts, and I knew my job inside and out.

I took some time to sit down and crunch the numbers. I had a choice: keep living a "normal" life and look for another job, or take a leap of faith and pursue my own path. I chose to pursue my own path—and that decision came with huge consequences. No steady income would be coming in to sustain my bills.

The first step was letting go of my car. I called the finance company and told them they could pick up my 2005 BMW 645 CI Convertible. I loved that car, but I knew it was for the best—and I knew I could achieve three times more if I put in the work. Next, I had to downgrade my living situation. At the time, I was in a high-rise apt in downtown Miami with a beautiful view—but I knew there was a bigger purpose for me, and I had to take the leap.

I found a place in Overtown, Florida—a neighborhood known for its challenges, including crime, drug activity, and other risks. It was one of the only affordable options close enough to downtown Miami. After much thought, I made the move: I gave back my BMW, bought a 2002 Audi station wagon with cash, and relocated to a studio apartment in the heart of Overtown that looked more like a storefront than a home.

I couldn't believe I was actually doing this. I was nervous, but I trusted that it was for the best for my growth. I knew God had me, and I understood that taking this leap was the first step toward creating something far greater than I could achieve by playing it safe.

Instead of looking for another job, I threw myself into the journey of entrepreneurship. I focused on building my IT consulting business from scratch, leveraging my skills, experience, and contacts. It wasn't easy—there were long hours, sacrifices, and moments of doubt—but I executed fast and stayed consistent. I took a leap of faith and started my IT company, **WilliamsTEK**, which is based on my family's last name

& by the end of that first year, I had tripled my income. I didn't just survive—I thrived.

This experience taught me the essence of entrepreneurship: taking risks, trusting yourself, and acting decisively, even when the outcome is uncertain. Playing it safe would have kept me comfortable, but it would never have allowed me to realize my full potential. Sometimes, you have to step into the unknown, make tough choices, and trust that your hard work and resilience will guide you to success.

When I got kicked out of my apartment, it wasn't just about money—I didn't have first month, last month, or security to move into another place immediately. My ex-girlfriend had falsely accused me of acts I didn't commit, and as a result, I had nowhere to go. I didn't know many people in Miami since I had just moved to the city. That's when I realized how important savings are—and how being with the wrong person can derail your future.

While I had nowhere to turn, I thought about my job and my co-worker, Nick, who sometimes worked remotely from Orlando. It was just the two of us on the floor, and we had built a system of trust and honor between us. I proposed that I handle the bulk of the work in the office while he managed all the admin tasks from home. He agreed, partly because he hated driving to Miami anyway. With this arrangement, I was able to sleep in the office at night until I figured out my next move.

The building I worked in was in downtown Miami, near shops, restaurants, and offices. One day, walking down Flagler Street, I noticed a lease sign: a office for $500. A lightbulb went off—I could afford this and save money while getting back on my feet. I applied and got approved. It wasn't a large space, but it was comfortable. Everything I needed was within walking distance, and while it didn't have a shower, there was a regular bathroom. I joined Youfit gym for $10 a month to work out and shower—a perfect temporary solution (shoutout to YouFit Gym).

Around the same time, I started my fashion line, Status Plus Fashions. During the day, I focused on tech work, and at night, the office became the hub for Status Plus Fashions: developing designs, creating mockups, sewing sample clothing, and even holding photoshoots. My good friend Craig would drive down from Orlando on the weekends, and we'd find models on the street to shoot with. Those weekends were some of the best memories—creative, exhausting, and exhilarating.

That period was about survival—but it was also about thriving even in adversity. My back was against the wall, but pressure pushed me to innovate, hustle harder, and maximize every resource I had. Those early struggles shaped the foundation of everything I've built since—both Williamstek and Status Plus Fashions. And it taught me a lesson I carry to this day: when you face challenges head-on, even on your worst day, you can still come out stronger.

So, as we move forward with this journey, we're not just building a brand—we're building a movement. A movement that inspires people to break free from fear and doubt. A movement that says no matter where you come from, no matter what you've been through, you can create the life you've always dreamed of. When people hear the message,

DREAMS IN THE MAKING

"Even on my worst day," they'll know it's more than just a slogan. It's a declaration of strength, resilience, and faith in the journey. And together, we'll prove that anything is possible when you refuse to play it safe.

The resilience I built through the toughest times of my life came from the grind—the constant, relentless hustle that never allowed me to stop. There's something powerful about the moments when you're stripped down to the basics. When everything is gone, you're forced to get creative, dig deep into your own strength, and find solutions where others might give up.

Like I said before, I wasn't always the perfect citizen, but I knew how to stop or cut things off when they went too far. Back in 2009, while in Atlanta, I found myself running with a crew of mixed personalities—some good, some so-so, and some just destructive. Even though I ran with them, I stayed true to myself and thought for myself. But eventually, some of the activities caught up to me, and that's how I ended up in jail.

When I got out, I had lost my place, and the crew I ran with took everything from the apartment we shared. I had nowhere to go, so I called my brother Randy. At the time, he lived in a small one-bedroom apartment with his girlfriend Nerissa and his dog in Norcross ga. He offered me the couch until I could get back on my feet. He didn't have to do it, but he did—and that's when I truly understood the value of family. Thank you, little brother—I owe you a lot.

I didn't have a car, and I didn't have money for much of anything. But that didn't stop me. I got a job, and my situation meant I had to walk everywhere—literally. From my brother's apartment at the back of the complex, I'd Walk half a mile to the entrance, catch the bus to the train, and then walk to work.

It was a grueling routine—waking up at 6 AM and getting home at 8 PM—but I never saw it as negative. It helped me get into great shape. With a food stamp card to eat, I kept my meals light: canned food, tuna fish, green peas, and water. I didn't want to put anything in my body that would slow me down or make me tired. It was tough, but I focused on the long-term goal. In just six months of hard work and hustle, I had a place of my own, a car, and a fully furnished apartment. I was determined to have it—and to get it.

That was the turning point. It was the direct result of not playing it safe—making the hard decisions, knowing each step would bring me closer to my vision. You have to keep pushing forward, even when everything feels stacked against you. Keep showing up, even when no one is watching, even when you're walking miles just to survive. It's not about the struggle—it's about what you make of it.

And that's where I stand today—grateful for every step of the journey. I refuse to sit back and wait for things to happen. I choose to swim, rather than sink, regardless of the obstacles, because with the gifts God has given me, I have what it takes to succeed.

For anyone listening, feeling like they're on their own journey of struggle or uncertainty—let me tell you this: it's in these moments that you find your true strength. The world may tell you it's too hard, that you can't make it, or that you should take the safe route. Don't listen. You have the power to create the life you want. Even on your worst day, you can rise and make something great of yourself. You are not defined by your circumstances, but by the decisions you make and the actions you take.

One thing I wish I could tell younger Maurice is this: Surround yourself with the right people. Find mentors who will push you, elevate you, and challenge you to be the best version of yourself. You can't do this journey alone. The right people make all the difference. They'll see in you what you might not see in yourself, and they'll guide you through the hard times.

I learned this the hard way. If I had stayed connected with the right group of people, I could have fast-tracked my success. Surround yourself with people who believe in you, and they'll help you recognize opportunities you might otherwise miss.

As we close this chapter, remember this: the journey you're on might not always be easy, but it's worth it. There's greatness in the grind and strength in the struggle. If you keep pushing and keep believing, you'll look back one day and realize just how far you've come.

No matter the challenges you face, no matter how tough it gets, know that you can make it. You have everything you need inside of you. Keep moving forward. Keep fighting. And even on your worst day, remember: you are destined for greatness.

CHAPTER
04
The Big Idea

Building a brand—especially one that lasts—always begins with a vision bigger than yourself. It starts with a big idea, the kind that gets inside you and won't let go. The kind that pushes you through obstacles, challenges, and doubts, even when the odds feel stacked against you.

For me, that idea came when I realized I didn't just want to design clothes. I wanted to create something that stood for more than fabric and logos—something that represented resilience, confidence, and a lifestyle. I wasn't chasing a product. I was building a movement.

The first step in that journey was surrounding myself with the right people, finding inspiration, and seeking guidance that could bring the vision to life. That search led me to Atlanta. At the time, I had just gone through a few setbacks and was trying to find my footing again. That's when I reconnected with someone from my past—Kelvin, better known as Blakka.

THE BIG IDEA

Life has a way of coming full circle. Blakka had once tricked me in a real estate deal, and normally that would've been the end of it. But in this case, he became an unlikely bridge to my next chapter. He owned a clothing store out in Stone Mountain, Georgia, and through him I met a man named Chilly-O.

Chilly-O would go on to be much more than a connection. He became a mentor—someone whose insight, energy, and guidance helped me sharpen my vision and begin turning that big idea from a dream into something real.

Chilly-O was already making waves in Atlanta with his clothing line. What set him apart was his signature touch—a simple safety pin fastened to the label of his hats, shirts, and other accessories. It was subtle, almost unassuming, yet it gave every piece an edge. That small detail transformed each item into something that felt personal, custom, and bold. I remember seeing it for the first time and thinking it was one of the coolest, most creative touches I had ever come across.

But it wasn't just his design. Chilly-O had stripes in the game—he'd earned respect working with legends like Outkast, the Dungeon Family, and a lineup of artists who shaped Atlanta's whole culture. His work wasn't just fashion; it was part of the city's heartbeat. Seeing people, I looked up to rocking his pieces lit a fire in me. That's when I knew—I couldn't just admire the movement from the sidelines. I had to build my own.

So, I stepped to him and laid out my vision for Status Plus Fashions. Back then, it was just words—a phrase I'd been saying for years to describe a mindset—but I had never put it on a shirt, never stamped it into the culture. Chilly-O listened, and instead of brushing me off, he embraced it. He dropped real game about the grind—fabric quality, branding, production timelines, pricing. He plugged me in with the right people—pattern makers, screen printers, manufacturers—and even pulled up with me to print shops when I needed guidance.

That's mentorship in its purest form—passing the torch, but making sure you're ready to carry the weight.

With Chilly-O's mentorship, I started grinding even harder on my own. Nights were spent locked in research, days were spent making calls, surfing the internet, and building relationships with both local and overseas manufacturers. I was learning the ropes piece by piece—how to move in this business, how to make connections that mattered, how to turn an idea into something real.

Eventually, I pulled the trigger on my first batch of samples. When that box landed, I ripped it open like a kid on Christmas morning. For the first time, I was holding Status Plus in my hands—not just a thought in my head or words on my tongue. It was real. I was ecstatic. The vision had weight now, and it all traced back to that safety pin and a mentor who was willing to lace me with game.

This was back in 2003–2004. Looking back now, two decades later, I'm humbled by how far I've come. Back then, Status Plus Fashions was nothing more than a collection of rough ideas rattling around in my mind. Today, it's a story I get to share with the world.

THE BIG IDEA

But ideas don't become movements without execution—and that's where another key player stepped in: Craig Walton Graham. Craig was my neighbor in New York, a graphic artist with raw talent and vision. He wasn't just good—he was exactly who I needed to translate the grind and the mindset of Status Plus into designs that could live on fabric. He helped me turn the vision into something tangible, something the world could finally see.

Craig wasn't just talented—he had a gift for pulling the vision out of my head and putting it on paper. I could spill out a mess of ideas, talking about themes, moods, and images, and he'd cut through it all with the right questions. Then he'd sit down and turn those raw thoughts into sharp, striking artwork that felt exactly like what I had imagined but couldn't draw myself.

I had a head full of concepts but no way to sketch them. That's where Craig came in. We'd spend hours on the phone hashing out logos, building mockups, and running through drafts until we landed on something that felt right. I'd describe the vision, and he'd bring it to life. Together, we created the original Status Plus logo and the first designs that gave the brand its identity.

For years, Craig and I worked side by side—creating, refining, and shaping the face of Status Plus Fashions. But building something from nothing takes more than talent; it takes time, sacrifice, and unshakable faith when the money isn't showing up. After years of grinding without real financial reward, the fire that fueled our partnership started to fade for him. He had a family, responsibilities, and other paths to follow. Eventually, he stepped back.

That's when the loneliness set in. The late-night calls were gone. The back-and-forth sketches, the rush of bouncing ideas—all of it faded. For the first time, I was carrying the vision alone. But instead of letting that break me, it made me hungrier. I knew if I didn't push forward, everything we built would disappear.

So, I embraced the solitude. I learned to sit with it, to let it sharpen me. The weight of the journey got heavier, but so did my drive. Loneliness taught me a valuable lesson: even if people fall off along the way, the vision is still mine to carry—and I refused to put it down.

Although our paths eventually diverged, I've always honored the role Craig played in bringing Status Plus Fashions to life. Even after he stepped away, his influence stayed stitched into the fabric of the brand. I kept the torch burning, pushing forward with the dream he helped spark. Status Plus Fashions wasn't just my idea—it was a shared vision shaped by the people who believed in it. And that's something I'll never forget.

When I moved from New York to Atlanta, the story kept evolving. I met new people, built stronger connections, and poured myself into nurturing the brand. Early on, I learned a hard truth: it takes more than passion to build something that lasts. It takes time, perseverance, and a sharp awareness of how the game works. You can't sell a product if nobody knows it exists.

THE BIG IDEA

At the start, I didn't have a business plan, a strategy, or a blueprint. What I had was belief—and excitement about what this brand could become. So, I did what I could with what I had. I made shirts and handed them out to people in my circle. I wasn't chasing profit at that moment; I was chasing recognition. Everyone I knew, everyone I respected, became a walking billboard. And it worked. The designs were fresh, people wanted to represent, and word started spreading.

What began as free shirts on the backs of friends quickly turned into conversations, connections, and credibility. Status Plus was no longer just an idea—it was becoming a name people recognized.

As I started thinking bigger, I knew the brand couldn't just live on the backs of friends rocking the shirts. If Status Plus was going to reach the next level, I needed real brand ambassadors. Not just people wearing the clothes, but people who embodied the mindset—people who lived the message, talked about it, and carried it into the right spaces. Ambassadors don't just put on the product; they represent the lifestyle, the story, and the culture behind it.

But here's the thing about building from the ground up: the hardest part isn't making the product; it's finding the right people to ride with you. That's where some of my toughest lessons came. Over the years, I worked with all kinds of people—some solid, some not so much—and I learned the hard way that if you don't know your target audience, you'll bleed money chasing results that never show up.

I put serious time and money into consultants and so-called marketing experts, only to realize they didn't understand the brand or the people it was meant for. Instead of connecting with the culture, they threw out generic ideas and "strategies" that never landed. More than once, I had people promise they could take Status Plus to the next level, but all they delivered were expensive invoices and campaigns that had nothing to do with the vision. The content didn't resonate, the message didn't connect, and the people we wanted to reach never heard it.

Those experiences taught me a truth I carry to this day: it's not enough to market—you have to connect.

That's the part most people don't get: you can be talented, creative, even skilled at your craft—but if you don't know who you're speaking to, all that effort gets wasted. And for me, the issue wasn't just the consultants. The truth was, I hadn't fully learned how to educate myself—and the people around me—on what the brand really stood for.

Knowing your avatar—your target audience—is everything. If you don't know who you're talking to, your message falls flat. It's like sending your mom a text meant for your cousin—it's out of place, it doesn't connect. So, I had to step back and ask myself the hard questions: *Who am I really speaking to? Who do I want carrying this flag? Who do I trust to represent Status Plus the way it was meant to be represented?* Once I got clear on those answers, the picture sharpened.

That's why I became so passionate about the brand ambassador program. You need people who don't just wear the clothes, but who live the mindset. People who understand the mission and represent it because they believe in it—not just because it looks good on them.

THE BIG IDEA

The first person to step into that role was DJ Epps. At the time, he was already moving heavy in the Miami music scene—hosting parties, breaking records, rocking crowds. When Epps threw on Status Plus, it wasn't just another shirt—it was a statement. He carried the brand into rooms I couldn't reach on my own, putting it in front of tastemakers and influencers who mattered. People saw him wearing it, repping it, and suddenly the conversation around Status Plus got louder.

That was the moment I saw the power of true ambassadors. When the right person believes in your vision, they don't just wear the brand—they amplify it.

In the early days, nothing was smooth. Plans blew up, partners tapped out, people got lazy, and there were nights I sat there wondering when will this pop off how can I make this pop off. There were moments when it felt like I was carrying the whole thing on my back with no support. But quitting? That was never on the table. This brand is my life—Status Plus, *Even on My Worst Day*—and I wasn't about to fold. This isn't just a hustle for me; it's a message the world needs to hear. So even when I was discouraged, even when it felt like nobody cared, I kept grinding. I believed in it too much to let it die.

That's the reality most people don't talk about. It's easy to walk away when nothing's moving. It's easy to tell yourself it wasn't meant to be. But if you really believe in what you're building, you've got to fight through those nights when doubt creeps in. On this journey, you've got to be your own hype man, your own biggest believer—because people will come and go. And when the dust settles, all you've really got is your vision.

Looking back, I know I was winging it. I had drive, but no real plan. No business model. No roadmap. I thought passion alone would carry me, but passion without strategy will drain your pockets and your spirit. I should've studied more, learned the game inside out, and built a tighter plan. Making money isn't impossible, but it's not magic either. It takes patience, structure, and mentors who won't sugarcoat the truth.

And I learned the hard way about investing in the brand. I spent thousands on consultants, branding, and marketing, thinking they were the answer. Most of it turned out to be smoke and mirrors. They didn't know my audience, they didn't feel the vision—they just sold me dreams and sent invoices. More than once, I got burned—money gone, time wasted, nothing to show for it. That kind of loss cuts deep. But instead of breaking me, it hardened me. It taught me to protect the vision and to only put my energy and resources where they truly matter.

There were times when I felt I'd been sold a dream by people who didn't really understand Status Plus. They put the brand out in ways that didn't align with what I was trying to build. Some of that was on me—I hadn't been clear enough about my vision—but it taught me how crucial it is to be specific about how you want your brand represented. It's not enough to trust just anyone with your vision. Over time I realized that knowing who you're speaking to and communicating clearly is everything. You have to set the tone, bring the right people on board and keep the brand true to what it stands for. That's a big part of building something that lasts.

THE BIG IDEA

Fast forward to 2012, after my move to Miami I decided to take part in a large event in Wynwood. Wynwood was an area that had once been a run-down industrial neighborhood plagued by drugs and crime, but over time it had been transformed into a thriving art district where everyone went to experience Miami's culture. One day I saw ads on social media for a Wynwood festival and thought: I have some dope designs, I have brand ambassadors and models, and my right-hand man Craig—who also happens to be a photographer. Why not try? So I applied, got approved to vend and paid the fee. That event became my first experience vending. The turnout was huge and the energy high; it gave me the confidence boost I needed. I had my booth, my models and my products, and people loved it. I made valuable connections and sold a lot of merchandise. That moment showed me it was possible to make it happen, even when the odds seemed stacked against me.

Now it feels like things have come full circle. In 2025 I did a relaunch in Wynwood, this time for Miami's 305 Day—a major celebration of the city's culture. I was able to participate with the help of world-famous DJ Epps, who has become a huge part of Status Plus brand and one of our biggest brand ambassadors. So, returning to Wynwood felt like coming home. To think my first major success happened there, and now I'm going back with a new vision, a new message and a stronger foundation—that's powerful.

Ever since I started this journey, people have told me how much they love the brand and ask why I slowed down with Status Plus. Everywhere I go they call me "Status" and ask, "Hey, what's going on with the brand? Why did you stop?" They never let me forget it. Every time someone sees me, they bring it up—and that's powerful. They're still waiting for me to blow this thing up. I have people who genuinely want to see me win, and that means a lot to me.

But life happens, and I've learned that my biggest setbacks have come from getting caught up in other people's visions and movements, from being distracted by other opportunities, and from being in relationships that didn't serve my purpose, passion or mission.

Knowing that people believe in you and your brand is huge. It's not just about building a business—it's about building a community around it. When friends or strangers ask what happened to Status Plus, it's less a question than a reminder. They're saying they care; they want to see me succeed. That kind of support keeps me going. It tells me that Status Plus isn't just about me; it's about everyone who resonates with the message and the vision.

Their encouragement reminds me why I started: to build something real, something that unites people and inspires them to push through. Every time somebody calls me "Status" or asks about the brand, it's a reminder that there's a community out there waiting. I'm not just selling clothes—I'm pushing a story, a mindset, a way of moving through life. Knowing people are still watching, still waiting for me to take it to the next level—that's fuel. It keeps me sharp, keeps me grinding, keeps me hungry.

But let me be real: every entrepreneur needs to understand the power of their circle. Who you keep around you will either build you up or bleed you dry. Too many times, I got caught up with the wrong crowd—

people who took what they could and vanished when it was my turn to lean. That kind of energy will kill your drive if you let it.

You've got to find your tribe. Not yes-men. Not clout chasers. Not people clapping for you in public but jealous in private. I'm talking about the ones who cheer when you win, who push you when you stall, who call you out when you're slipping. Your tribe should be mentors, peers, and friends who share the vision, speak the truth, and want to see you win just as bad as you want it yourself. With the right people in your corner, you can take punches, weather storms, and keep swinging when everybody else expects you to fold.

You don't need takers. You need people who pour into you—who bring ideas, connections, and encouragement without being asked. People who see your potential and refuse to let you waste it. Those are the ones who'll walk with you, fight for you, and remind you of your "why" when you're one step away from quitting.

The right circle doesn't wait for instructions—they move. They make plays, they hold you accountable, and they don't let you forget the mission. So, my advice to any young hustler out there: **find your tribe.** Find the people who believe in your vision, ride with your mission, and want to see you eat. Because when you lock in with the right crew—the ones who challenge you, push you, and keep you on your toes—you'll realize there's no limit to how far you can go.

CHAPTER 05
Built Different

When people see the title *Even On My Worst Day*, I don't just want them to read it—I want them to feel it. I want it to cut deeper than emotion, to hit them in a place where they can't ignore it. A reminder that they're not alone in the struggle.

Because no matter what you're going through, somebody else has carried that same weight. Somebody else has felt that same fear, that same disappointment—and still found a way to rise. That's what this title stands for: hope.

Hope that tomorrow can look different. Hope that pain doesn't get the last word. Hope that the worst days don't define your entire life.

But I don't just want people to feel hope—I want them to feel strength. To know that even when life hits hard, you can hit back harder. To realize that bad days are just that—days. They come, they go, and they pass. And when the smoke clears, you'll still be standing.

I can say that with confidence because I've lived it. I've faced days so heavy they made me question everything. Days that made me wonder if I'd ever bounce back. But here's the truth: I didn't just survive those days—I was forged by them.

That's what makes us different. It's not the easy moments, not the trophies, not the applause. It's the nights when everything is stacked against you, and you still choose to fight. That's where strength is born.

I'll never forget one of the lowest points in my life—walking out of jail with nothing but the clothes on my back. No money. No home. No clear path forward. Just me, my thoughts, and a brother who opened his door when I had nowhere else to go. In that moment, that felt like everything.

I still remember sitting in that cell, staring at the clock like it was taunting me. Time dragged so slow it felt like it had stopped. Every hour was heavy, every second felt like a question mark. *Who am I? How did I get here? What will life look like if I get another shot?*

I was surrounded by noise, negativity, and distractions, but in that darkness, I found clarity. I started talking to God. I started writing. Every day, I grabbed a notebook and mapped out a plan—business ideas, names of people I needed to connect with, ways to get my body right, how to take Status Plus from a dream in my head to a brand the world would know.

And in that moment, I made myself a promise:

"If I got another chance, I'm not wasting it. I'm going to do this right."

That notebook became my blueprint for redemption. And when I walked out, I followed that blueprint step by step. Not because it was easy—but because it was necessary.

See, something happens when you hit rock bottom. The noise fades. The masks come off. And you're left face-to-face with your true self. You learn who you really are, what you're willing to fight for, and what you can live without.

Rock bottom will break some people. But if you let it, it can also build you. That pain, that silence, that loss—it can mold you into someone stronger. Someone wiser. Someone who knows how to stand when everything around them says sit down. Someone built different.

That's what happened to me. I stopped chasing validation and started chasing purpose. I stopped running from my past and started building my future. Every day was just a small step, but each step mattered. And little by little, the man I saw on those pages became the man I saw in the mirror.

A Message to the Ones Still Inside

If I could speak directly to the men and women still incarcerated—especially those living through their worst days behind those walls—I'd tell you this: there is always light at the end of the tunnel. Always.

But here's the truth—you've got to protect your mind. That's your most valuable asset. The bars can only hold your body, but it's the negativity, the gossip, the nonsense—that's what can trap your spirit longer than any sentence ever could. Stay away from the knuckleheads.

Stay away from the drama. Guard your peace like your life depends on it—because it does.

Use that time wisely. Think. Reflect. Get to know the real you—the one underneath the mistakes, the pain, and the pressure. Every single day, write down your plan. Don't wait until you're free to start building your future. Start now. Behind those walls, you have something rare: time. No distractions. No outside noise. Use it.

Sit with yourself. Talk to God. Be honest about your past, your pain, and your dreams. Write it all down. Build a blueprint the future you can follow, step by step.

Because your day will come. And when that door opens—when you finally walk out—you don't walk out broken. You don't walk out lost. You walk out ready. You walk out prepared. You walk out built to win.

The Power of Community

I've always believed in giving back. That's why I talk so much about going into schools, mentoring youth, and showing up for my community—because I know what it feels like when nobody shows up for you. I know how powerful it is when just one person steps in and makes a difference.

We have to teach the next generation that life is not a game. It's real. Every decision carries weight—good or bad. The people you keep around you, the voices you listen to, the energy you allow into your life—it all shapes your future.

Too many young people are being led by people who don't even know the truth themselves. It's like a game of telephone: by the time the message gets to them, it's twisted and broken. That's why mentorship matters. That's why authentic voices matter.

We need people who've lived it, stumbled, been written off—and still made it back. Not just with scars, but with solutions. People who can say: *"I've been where you are, and I know the way forward."*

That's why I show up. Because I want the next person coming up behind me to know that success doesn't mean perfection. Success means perseverance. It means progress. It means pushing through your worst days and still finding a way to keep moving.

What I'd Tell My Younger Self

If I could go back in time and speak to the younger versions of me, here's what I'd say:

To 10–12-year-old Maurice:
Be curious. Be adventurous. Don't be afraid to ask questions, and don't be afraid to stand out. Listen to the voices that truly care—your mom, your grandparents, your uncles your aunts, & your teachers. Pay attention to what lights you up inside, because those sparks are clues to your purpose. And never forget—your life matters.

To 16-year-old Maurice:
Watch the company you keep. Your friends will shape your future more than you realize. Just because someone's popular or funny doesn't mean they're good for you. Don't fall for the hype. Be bold enough to walk away from the crowd if that's what it takes to save your life. Integrity might not look cool at sixteen, but it'll keep you alive at thirty.

To 21–25-year-old Maurice:

Stay locked in. Master your craft. Travel. Try new things. Make mistakes, but learn quickly, because time is more valuable than money. Don't let women, distractions, or the desire to be liked pull you off your mission. That trap is easy to fall into and hard to climb out of. Invest in your vision instead. Learn money. Learn business. Build something that lasts. Become the kind of man your future self can depend on.

To Every Man Who Feels Like It's Too Late

You might be reading this thinking, "Man, I already messed up. I wasted time. I should be farther by now."

I know that feeling—I've been there. But hear me clearly: **you are not too late.**

As long as you're breathing, your story isn't finished.

The only thing that makes me different is simple—I refused to quit. I've taken losses, faced setbacks, been embarrassed, even failed in public. But I never let those moments define me. Why? Because I believed that even on my worst day, I still had value. And so do you.

You can still win. You can still heal. You can still rebuild. But it starts with the work.

Silence the noise. Step away from social media. Turn off the TV. Stop comparing your life to somebody else's highlight reel. If you have to, disappear for a season—lock in and focus only on building, learning, and growing.

Fall in love with becoming the man you were always meant to be. Educate yourself. Read daily. Watch things that expand your mind. Take walks alone and reflect. Strengthen your spirit. Surround yourself with people who pour into you—not just hype, but substance. Study the ones who've done what you dream of doing, and let them mentor you—even from a distance.

You don't need the perfect plan—you just need discipline. Start where you are. Use what you have. Commit to the long game.

Because when you move with intention, doors open.
When you stay consistent, opportunities find you.
And when you believe in yourself, nothing can stop you.

Why I Keep Showing Up

I don't share these stories to brag—I share them to build. Because right now, somebody feels hopeless. Somebody is sitting in the dark convinced there's no way out. And I know that feeling.

But I also know what's possible. I know you can start with nothing and still become something. I know you can lose everything and still discover who you really are. I know you can be written off, overlooked, counted out—and still rise back stronger than ever.

You don't have to be perfect—you just have to keep going.

Remember this: situations are temporary, never permanent. And even on your worst day, **your Status is Plus.** That's what makes you different.

CHAPTER 06

The Money Shift

Before I ever made real money, nobody ever sat me down to talk about it. Growing up, money wasn't a topic in the house. We didn't talk about savings, credit, or investments. Nobody explained budgets, ownership, or how to build wealth. We just lived day to day.

If the lights got cut off, we waited until they came back on. If we couldn't afford something, we just went without. There was no breakdown, no strategy—just survival. All I knew was that money was something we didn't have enough of.

It wasn't until I got older that I realized how little I actually knew about money. And the truth is, I didn't learn it in my own community. I learned it by being around people who had it.

Like I said before, I went to a school where most of my classmates were white. I'll never forget the difference. I saw sixteen-year-old kids and kids who were pulling up to school in Mercedes and Lexus's—cars their parents bought them. Meanwhile, I was just trying not to miss the bus in the morning.

That was wild to me. But instead of just being jealous, I started paying attention. I asked questions. I studied their habits. I noticed what was normal for them that felt like a dream for me. And little by little, my perspective on money began to shift.

One moment that changed everything was when I got invited to my brother Randy's friend's birthday party in Dix Hills. His family was Indian, and his father was a doctor. I'll never forget walking through those doors and feeling like I had just stepped into another world.

There was a swimming pool inside the house. I had never seen anything like that in my life. Maids moving around. Butlers serving food. Fancy dishes laid out like it was a five-star restaurant. It felt like a movie scene. That was the first time I said to myself: *"I want to live like this."*

From that day forward, I couldn't unsee it. Another friend had housekeepers. Another had cooks. Everywhere I turned, I saw wealth, privilege, and comfort that I had never known. And instead of making me bitter, it lit a fire in me. I didn't know how I was going to get there, but I knew I wanted that kind of life. I just had to figure out the blueprint.

At the age of 13 my very first real job was delivering newspapers. Back then, there was no internet like today—everything was print, and people depended on those papers being at their doorstep. I found the job flipping through the classifieds in the newspaper. My mother helped make it happen—she'd drive me to the plant to pick up the *Newsday* newspapers, and I'd spend Friday nights putting them together downstair in my house so I could deliver them at the crack of dawn Saturday morning.

Thank you, Ma. That was the first step. The grind started there.

Every Friday night, I'd stay up almost all-night bagging newspapers for my route. I was too young to drive back then, so I strapped baskets to each side of my bike, loaded them to the top, and rode through the neighborhood house by house swinging newspapers in the driveway.

It wasn't easy. Sometimes I got chased by dogs. Other times I got caught in the rain—or even snow. But no matter what, those papers got delivered. That route taught me the value of hard work, discipline, and earning a paycheck. And even though it was physical work, I can look back now and appreciate it—it kept me sharp, it kept me focused, and it kept me in shape.

My second job came when I was sixteen, working at Burger King. Flipping burgers might not sound like much, but for me it was another step toward independence. I was finally making my own money, buying my own clothes, and getting the things I wanted without having to ask. It felt good to provide for myself.

But that job didn't last long. One day the manager told me I had to shave before my shift. I had never shaved before, didn't trust the razor, and honestly didn't know what I was doing. On top of that, the razor they had looked rusty and dirty. I wasn't about to put that on my face.

THE MONEY SHIFT

I called my brother Derrick to ask how to even shave—what direction to move the blade, what to avoid. He broke it down and told me something real: *"Our hair is different. If you don't do it right, you'll tear up your skin and break out in bumps. Especially with a cheap razor. Don't let them push you into messing up your face just to flip burgers."*

That stuck with me. So, I refused. The manager didn't want to hear it. He sent me home, and just like that, my time at Burger King was done.

Even though it was short-lived, I walked away with a lesson: money gave me freedom, but I didn't want anyone else controlling my future.

After Burger King, I landed a job at Toys "R" Us, still sixteen. But that job was fun. I was stocking shelves, working overnight doing inventory, and clocking in as much overtime as I wanted. For the first time, I started seeing decent checks. At $7 an hour, I was pulling in $500—sometimes even $800. At sixteen, that felt like real money. And it felt even better knowing I earned it myself.

But the real shift came when I got into the phone company—Bell Atlantic—in 1998. I was making $9 an hour, and with time and a half I was hitting $21. The overtime was unlimited. I was grinding, putting in hours whenever I could. At eighteen I had the energy and the hunger. I didn't care what time it was—I was chasing checks. And those checks were hitting $2,000 to $3,000 every pay period. That was life-changing money for me at the time.

By then, I had already bought my first car at seventeen. My mother made me a deal: if I came up with half, she and my grandmother would cover the rest. That was all I needed to hear—it was on. I had my eye on a 1987 Honda Accord, and from that moment, every shift, every overtime hour, every dollar I saved was for one thing—getting that car.

And when I finally got behind that wheel, it wasn't just about driving. It was about independence. It was proof that my hustle was paying off.

That drive taught me discipline. It showed me that money wasn't just about survival—it was about setting goals, working toward them, and creating freedom.

The job environment at Bell Atlantic shaped me in ways I didn't expect. I was surrounded by a lot of white folks, and the conversations were different. They weren't talking about just scraping by—they talked about summer homes, stocks, and family vacations. That was the first time I heard money being discussed in terms of building, investing, and creating a lifestyle—not just paying bills.

I gravitated toward it. I listened closely. I picked up the language. I studied their habits. And I realized something important: if I wanted what they had, I couldn't just dream about it—I had to adopt the mindset and the moves that built it.

After a few years with Bell Atlantic, I got an opportunity that changed everything. The company was offering spots for a government contract job at Brooklyn College campus. Everybody wanted in. I understood why. The Government worked different—it was what they called a prevailing wage job. That meant the pay rate wasn't just good—it was

THE MONEY SHIFT

life-changing. For me, it meant jumping from around $25 an hour to $62 an hour.

At nineteen, that number hit me like a shockwave. Sixty-two dollars an hour? It felt unreal—like I had just hit the jackpot.

But it didn't just fall into my lap. I had to do everything in my playbook to get selected. I carried myself professionally. I made sure my work spoke louder than anything else. I stayed clear of the knucklehead behavior that could've cost me the opportunity. And when the time came, I got the call—I was chosen.

That moment proved something to me: preparation pays off. With Hard work, discipline, and consistency. It positions you for the opportunity when it shows up.

When those first checks started coming in from that government job, life got wild. I went out and bought myself a Lexus SC400—one of the hottest whips on the street at the time, the same car you'd see in music videos. Nineteen years old, riding luxury. And to top it off, I had a home built in Atlanta.

On the outside, it looked like I was winning. To some people, I looked untouchable. In fact, people thought I was a drug dealer because of how fast I came up.

But here's the truth: I had money, but I didn't have knowledge. Nobody ever taught me about taxes, savings, or property management. I was young, reckless, and financially uneducated. I maxed out credit cards. I overspent. I stretched myself too thin.

And eventually, it all came crashing down.

Foreclosure. Repossession. Bad credit.

I went from living big to sleeping on my brother's couch. That was one of my worst days.

But like every chapter in this book says—*even on my worst day, I wasn't done.* That fall from financial grace became my teacher. I humbled myself and started studying. I went to credit school. I learned about business structures. I watched videos. I found mentors. And I made a commitment: the next time around, I was going to do it differently.

That season taught me everything I didn't know the first time. Now, my perspective on money is completely different. Money is a tool. It's not meant for flexing—it's meant for building, investing, multiplying.

These days, everything I buy has to serve a purpose. If it's not making me money or saving me time, I don't want it. Money isn't evil. People just misuse it. We fear what we don't understand—and growing up, I didn't understand money.

Now, I do.

My Advice

Keep your credit clean. Always have savings. Build multiple streams of income. Never depend on just one job—I've been laid off, fired, downsized, you name it. That taught me one thing: you have to stay ready.

Always be thinking about how to reinvent yourself. Learn to sell something. Teach something. Create something of value. And if selling isn't your strength, partner with someone who can. Collaborate. Use your creativity. Use your hustle.

And when it comes to hearing "no"? Get used to it. Keep moving until you get the "yes." Doubt will come. People will question you. That's part of the game.

But here's what I know: if the cavemen could survive with nothing but sticks and rocks, there's no excuse for us not to win with the resources we have today. That's the mindset I live by.

We've gotten soft because life got easier. But I keep my mentality sharp—like the lion and the gazelle. Both wake up knowing one thing: they have to run to survive. One runs to eat. The other runs to live. That's the urgency we need every single day.

That's how you survive. That's how you thrive. That's how you win.

Even on your worst day, you still have the power to shift your mindset, rebuild your finances, and create a legacy. The only question is: **how bad do you want it?**

After I recovered from that financial fall—the maxed-out credit cards, the foreclosure, the repossessions—I had to take a hard look in the mirror and ask myself one serious question: *What was it all for?*

I had tasted money. I had tasted the lifestyle. I knew the high of fast success. But what good is success if you don't know how to sustain it? What's the point of making it if you can't multiply it?

That's when I began to understand: true wealth isn't just about money.

Wealth is about **legacy**—building something that outlives you.

Wealth is about **ownership**—controlling your time, your assets, your future.

Wealth is about **freedom**—the ability to move how you want, when you want.

And more than anything, wealth is about **relationships**—surrounding yourself with people who pour into you, challenge you, and push you forward.

That shift in perspective changed everything. I stopped chasing just the dollar, and I started chasing impact, structure, and long-term stability.

That's when I realized I needed to get serious about collaboration. For too long, I tried to do everything myself. I thought asking for help made me look weak. I thought building alone would protect me from betrayal and disappointment.

But the truth is, isolation limits your impact. You can only go so far by yourself. Partnerships—when they're done right—elevate everything.

The hard lesson I had to learn was this: **not everybody deserves access to your vision.** Just because someone is close to you doesn't mean they're qualified to build with you. Loyalty is one thing—but alignment is everything.

Too many of us get caught up trying to bring everybody with us—friends, family, people from the block. And sometimes, it works. But most of the time, it doesn't. Because if people don't share your discipline, your vision, and your work ethic, you're dragging dead weight. And dead weight kills momentum.

You need partners who think long-term. People who aren't afraid to take the stairs. People who understand delayed gratification. Because when you build with integrity, it lasts.

I started looking at collaboration differently. Not just, *"Can you do this for me?"* but, *"Do we build the same way? Do we see the same future?"* The right partnership isn't just about what someone brings to the table—it's about shared values, shared strategy, and shared responsibility.

That's where the real money is.

When I was younger, I thought fast money was real money. But I learned the hard way that quick money comes with quick problems. Now, my focus is on building **sustainable income streams**—the kind that grow, compound, and create freedom for the long game.

It also means building teams and putting systems in place so the money doesn't stop if I take a break—or even if I step away completely. Because real wealth isn't tied to how many hours you can grind in a day. Real wealth is creating something that runs, produces, and multiplies—even without you.

That shift didn't happen overnight. It came from loss. From lessons. From the hunger to do better—not just for me, but for the people coming behind me.

I don't just want to have money. I want to build wealth that outlives me. And that kind of wealth isn't built on hype or shortcuts—it's built on wisdom.

You don't need ten side hustles. You need two or three focused income streams—the kind that grow with structure, vision, and strong partnerships. One stream can fund your life. The others can fund your legacy.

One of the biggest lies the world tells you is that money is the goal. Nah. Discipline is the goal.

Discipline builds money.
Discipline keeps money.
Discipline multiplies money.

You can hand $100,000 to an undisciplined man and watch it disappear in 30 days. But give $10,000 to a disciplined man with a strategy, and he'll find a way to flip it ten times over.

Discipline is saying *no* when everyone else is saying *yes*.
Discipline is stacking when everyone else is stunting.
Discipline is going home early to study, build, and rest instead of blowing money in the club trying to impress people who don't even care about you.

I had to learn to delay gratification. Just because I can afford something doesn't mean I need it. Just because an opportunity pops up doesn't mean it's meant for me.

Discipline gave me peace.

Discipline gave me options.

Discipline gave me a future.

And here's the truth: if your money doesn't have a purpose, it will disappear. If you don't have a plan for your money, trust me—somebody else will make one for you.

That's why I no longer chase trends. I don't jump at every shiny offer. I'm in this for the long game. I'm building something my kids' kids can eat off of.

Now, every dollar I make has a job. Every partnership I form has a goal. Every project I take on has a purpose. Because I'm not here to impress anyone—I'm here to leave something behind that actually matters.

For me, that means **investing**—in real estate, in businesses, in people, in the stock market. In assets that appreciate, not depreciate.

And when I partner with someone, I ask one simple question: *How does this help us both grow?* Because if one person is winning and the other is draining, that's not a partnership—that's a problem.

One of my biggest passions now is teaching young people the lessons I wish I knew earlier. I didn't grow up with financial literacy. Nobody taught me how to budget, how to invest, or how to use credit wisely. I had to bump my head, take losses, and learn the hard way before I finally understood how money really works.

But the younger generation doesn't have to repeat those same mistakes. That's why I talk to kids in schools. That's why I mentor young men. That's why I show up at programs and events. Because I want to help break the cycle.

Too many of us are stuck in survival mode when we were meant to thrive. Too many of us are working hard, but not working smart. Too many of us are chasing money instead of learning how to make money chase us—through smart investments, passive income, and ownership.

We need to start normalizing these conversations—credit, business structure, investment portfolios, generational wealth. Not just in boardrooms, but in barbershops, living rooms, and classrooms.

- If you want to change your money, change your mindset.
- If you want to change your family's future, change what you teach them today.

Build smart. Build together.

Because money doesn't change you—it reveals you. And what it revealed in me was this: I'm a builder. I'm a visionary. I'm a leader. But I'm also a man who made mistakes. I've been broke. I've been careless. I've had it all and lost it. But I've also learned, bounced back, and built better.

I've gone from sleeping on a couch to closing deals in boardrooms.
From foreclosure notices to property ownership.
From maxed-out credit cards to multiple streams of income.

Not because I'm special—but because I refused to let my worst days define me.

And you can too. Collaborate. Partner wisely. Learn constantly. Spend intentionally. Invest purposefully. Lead with discipline.

That's how you shift from chasing the bag to building the vault.

Your story's not over. The comeback will always be greater than the setback—especially when you're built different.

CHAPTER
07

Collaboration Over Competition

Collaboration is one of those words that gets tossed around in business and branding circles like it's just another buzzword. But for me? Collaboration is much deeper than simply working together.

It's about **vision.**

It's about **alignment.**

It's about **building something bigger than either person could create alone.**

When I collaborate, I'm not just doing it for clout or connections. I'm aligning with someone to push a greater purpose—whether that's building brand awareness, generating revenue, creating legacy, or simply delivering a powerful message to the world.

At the core, it has to be **mutually beneficial.** We both have to win. If I eat, you eat. That's how I move.

COLLABORATION OVER COMPETITION

Throughout my journey, I've had collaborations that turned into incredible experiences—projects that elevated my brand, my business, and my mindset. But I've also had collaborations that taught me hard lessons about what not to do. Honestly, both types shaped how I move today.

One of the best examples came when I first moved to Miami. I didn't know anyone yet, and I had just launched **Swag Rags**—an extension of the Status Plus brand.

To give you an idea, imagine if a scarf and a towel had a baby—that's a Swag Rag. I called it the "look good, feel good" fashion towel. Part design, part function—it kept you fresh while also looking like part of your outfit. (We'll dive deeper into the full Swag Rag story in another book.)

At that time, I was hungry to connect. I started checking Eventbrite for networking events, and that's how I ended up in Brickell going to a day party at Flanigan's, hosted by none other than Jim Jones.

That day changed everything.

In the middle of the party, I noticed world-famous **DJ Epps** on stage. The energy was crazy—he had the crowd moving, the sun was blazing, and he was hyping everybody up while dripping sweat under that Miami heat. That's when it hit me: *this product is perfect for him.*

Without hesitation, I walked straight up to the DJ booth, introduced myself, and said,
"Yo, I got something for you."

He looked at me like, "What you got?"

EVEN ON MY WORST DAY

I didn't even bother explaining. I just pulled it out and showed him.

His response?
"Yeah. I definitely need that."

Right there, I handed him a sample. That was always my thing—**I walked with product everywhere I went. Always ready.**

I gave him my number and told him to hit me up. And guess what? He did.

From that day forward, Epps turned out to be one of the most genuine and consistent brand ambassadors I've ever had. He rocked with me from day one—no ego, no politics, just pure support. He wore the product, told his people about it, and helped spread the word about the brand in ways I couldn't have done alone.

That experience taught me something powerful:
real collaboration isn't about transactions—it's about relationships.

People will show up when they think you can give them something, but the real ones? They stay consistent whether the cameras are on or not. Epps was one of those people. And that connection reminded me why I move the way I do—because when you build with the right people, it's never competition. It's elevation.

Over time, I made Epps custom rags, custom shirts—whatever he needed, I had him covered. And he returned the energy tenfold. Because of Epps, new doors opened. Connections were made. Opportunities came my way that I never could've planned for. That's a collaboration I'll always be grateful for.

COLLABORATION OVER COMPETITION

But not every partnership works out that way.

There was another time I tried to collaborate with someone with a bigger name—a well-known sports commentator for the Miami Heat, **Jason Jackson**, better known as "Jax" in the sports world. I met him through a mutual friend named **Will** from Minnesota. Will was a true sports fanatic—wherever his Vikings played, he was there. We got close, and through him, I got introduced to his circle. I was impressed by the athletes and sports figures he knew, and one of them happened to be Jax.

When Jax and I first met, we clicked instantly. He was cool, humble, and easy to vibe with. That's what sparked the idea to design a **custom Swag Rag** around his brand. Jax was a big personality—always on TV, always representing Miami—and I thought, *If I can connect my product with him, maybe it could open doors and even get the Swag Rag into the arena.*

He loved the concept and agreed to move forward. I brought in my designer Craig, and together we went back and forth on ideas until we landed on something special—a Swag Rag with "Jax" boldly printed across the middle and the phrase **"It's Time to Ball"** underneath.

We even did a photo shoot and produced a batch of the rags. At that point, I thought we had a game plan—a collaboration that could really take off.

But when the campaign launched, things didn't move how I expected. On my side, we were pushing hard, but our reach and resources were limited. On his side, there wasn't much movement at all. Without equal energy and effort, the momentum faded.

The product sat.
The connection faded.
The potential fizzled out.

It wasn't that anyone had bad intentions—it just wasn't structured right. The follow-through wasn't there. And that's when I learned the difference between a **cool idea** and a **strategic collaboration**. One moves. The other stalls.

Fast Forward to Invest Fest

Invest Fest is a platform created by the founders of the **Earn Your Leisure** podcast—a show I follow heavy. Their mission has always been about empowering our culture through financial literacy, wealth building, and ownership—but in a way that feels *real* and *relatable*.

What started as a podcast evolved into a full-blown movement—and eventually into one of the biggest festivals in our community.

Invest Fest brings together Black and Brown entrepreneurs, creators, and visionaries from all over the world to learn about financial independence and generational wealth. Since stepping into the mainstream, the Earn Your Leisure team has built a powerhouse brand that not only educates but also inspires people to take control of their money, their mindset, and their legacy.

Invest Fest isn't just an event—it's an **experience**.
It's about shifting how we see money.
It's about ownership, empowerment, and collaboration on a higher level.

COLLABORATION OVER COMPETITION

The year 2024 I finally made it to **Invest Fest**, it was held at the **Georgia World Congress Center**—a massive space overflowing with energy, culture, and opportunity. Inside was the **Marketplace**, a hub packed wall to wall with vendors of every kind. You had food, fashion, services, and educators—people sharing knowledge, dropping gems, and giving game. It wasn't just shopping; it was one of the most powerful networking spaces I'd ever experienced.

I missed the first year of Invest Fest, but I promised myself I wouldn't miss the next one. I told my boy, OG "We need to get out there. We need to build. We need to connect." I wasn't even focused on making sales—I was focused on finding **solutions**.

At that time, I had brands, ideas, and value—but I needed **protection**. Legal ownership. Trademark coverage. Something that made what I built *official.*

So, I walked that marketplace like a man on a mission.

That's when I stumbled across a booth and met **Genevieve Carvil-Harris**. She was there helping her friend with a pitch competition. At first, I thought it was just another gimmick—you know, those setups where people try to get you to sign up for "big exposure" or "cash prizes," only for it to turn into endless spam emails and robocalls. I almost kept it moving.

But something told me to stop. I asked, "So what do you do?"

She smiled and said she helped entrepreneurs. She even helped to educate them about the importance of **preparing and protecting their trademarks.**

I'll be honest—I didn't believe her at first. I said, "You don't look like you do anything with trademarks. You're up here trying to get people to sing for a pitch competition—and now you telling me you work with entrepreneurs?"

But the more she talked, the more it clicked. She answered every question with confidence—like someone who knew exactly what she was doing. Then she said something that stopped me cold: **she lived in Florida.** Just like me.

I laughed and said, "Ain't no way I came all the way to Atlanta to find the exact person I needed—who lives in my own state." That's when I knew it wasn't coincidence.

I told her, "We working as soon as I get back."

And we did.

From that one connection came more than just business help—it sparked a complete **vision reset.**

She invited me to a private mastermind. At first, I almost didn't go. I figured it'd be another surface-level networking event with no real follow-up. But something in me said, *show up anyway.*

When I walked in, I knew this was different. Gen and her husband, **Brian**—who's now a good friend of mine—were sitting on stage in chairs that looked like something a king and queen would sit on in their castle. The room was arranged with tables forming a big rectangle, and I took a seat among strangers. Then Gen explained that she had personally **hand-picked** everyone in that room.

This wasn't just another event.
This was **intentional.**
Every person there had purpose—and I was one of them.

We Went Around the Room

We went around introducing ourselves—sharing who we were, what we did, and why we were there. Then the event officially began.

When **Gen** started speaking, everything changed. The clarity in her words, the confidence in her tone, the power behind her presence—it all hit me at once.

I was no longer in disbelief.
In that moment, she made me a believer.

Through all my collaborations—some that worked, some that didn't—I finally found clarity.

Before, I had a **brand**, but I didn't have a **message**.
I had **products**, but not an **audience**.
I had **passion**, but not **direction**.

I knew what I stood for, but I didn't know how to communicate it in a way that moved people. I felt it inside—but I didn't know how to project it outside.

Now, I get it.

Now, I can speak to people in a way that connects—because I understand who they are, what they need, and how I can show up for them.

This book is part of that evolution.
It's more than a memoir—it's a **movement**.

It's me saying:

"Even on your worst day, you still matter.
Your story still matters.
And your brand—your identity—is still powerful."

Calling All Ambassadors

If you believe in this message—if you've been through some things and made it out stronger on the other side—then I want you to consider becoming a **Brand Ambassador** for the *Status Plus: Even On My Worst Day* campaign.

I'm looking for people who:

- Believe in the mission.
- Understand the power of resilience.
- Want to be a voice for others.
- Are ready to share this message within their own circles, communities, and platforms.

If that's you, then you already know—
you don't have to be perfect.
You just have to be **real**.

We'll include a link in this book where you can apply to join the ambassador community.

This isn't about hype.
It's about **impact**.

Final Words: Even On My Worst Day...

What I've learned through all of this is simple—but powerful:

Even on my worst day, I'm still capable.
Even on my worst day, I can still collaborate.
Even on my worst day, my status is **plus**.

People's opinions don't define me.
Obstacles don't stop me.
Losses don't break me.

And if I can come back from the things I've been through—
so can you.

So let's keep building.
Let's keep collaborating.
Let's keep growing.

Together.

REFLECTIONS

Mother of the Author
Faith in the Cold

One of my worst days was when we ran out of oil in the cold of winter. There was no heat to warm the house. One of my four sons, Derrick, had to ride his bicycle to the gas station to get some kerosene for our kerosene heater so we could have a little warmth in certain parts of the house. That heat would last us just long enough to make it through the night until the next day when we could get an oil delivery for the tank. I chose not to get stressed out or worry about what to do. We were able to make it through the night with some heat — thanks be to God for that kerosene heater.

We all bundled up together, my four sons and I, to stay warm. It wasn't comfortable, but it was love that kept us together, and faith that got us through. We made it through that night. If you ever face your own "worst day," remember this: with God, all things are possible. Have faith, pray, and believe in the Word of God. He will answer your prayers — just as He did for my four sons and me.

REFLECTIONS

Craigs Graham

Finding Beauty Beyond the Breaking Point

There are moments in life that shake us to our core—moments that make us question everything we thought we knew about ourselves, our future, and the people we love. For me, one of those "worst day" moments came when my wife of seventeen years decided she wanted a divorce. In that instant, everything I had built my world around seemed to crumble. The foundation of family, stability, and partnership I had counted on was suddenly gone.

But here's the truth I've learned since then: even in the hardest seasons, life still holds beauty. That pain became a turning point—one that reshaped my mindset, my faith, and my sense of purpose. The future I had imagined disappeared, but in its place came the opportunity to build something new. I made the decision to get excited about life again, to dream again, and to focus on what my new future could look like.

I pushed through because I knew I had no other choice. Giving up was never an option. Even when the weight of loneliness and disappointment pressed in, I reminded myself that life—no matter how difficult—was still worth living. There's a strange kind of grace that meets you in the hard places, if you're willing to look for it.

To anyone reading this who may be facing their own "worst day," I want to leave you with this: look for the beauty in life every single day. It's there—in a sunrise, a child's laughter, or even in the quiet strength that keeps you breathing when your heart is breaking. Take care of yourself, because the ones who love you need you to keep going. Keep your head up, even when it feels easier to hang it low.

Your story isn't over yet. Sometimes the ending you didn't expect becomes the beginning you didn't know you needed.

DJ Epps' Reflection
When the Music Stopped

One of my worst-day moments came when the pandemic hit, and everything suddenly shut down; the clubs, the crowds, the energy. For the first time in decades, I didn't know what to do next. My life has always been about movement, sound, and connection. Then, overnight, silence. I didn't know where my next income would come from or how I'd survive without doing what I knew best. But looking back, that season was more than just a shutdown — it was a reset. For over two or three decades, I had been grinding non-stop. The pandemic forced me to stop and rest — to give my body, mind, and soul a break. It shaped my mindset, strengthened my faith, and taught me to eliminate anything that didn't serve my purpose — the negativity, the fake friends, the noise. I learned that rest is part of growth, and sometimes God pauses your plans to prepare your purpose.

What helped me push through was the Almighty God. Some people forget to go to church or pray, but in that quiet season, I found my strength in faith. Even when I thought about giving up DJing to do something else, my spirit reminded me that the world still needs a DJ Epps — that what I create brings joy, and that's a calling worth continuing. So,

REFLECTIONS

if you're facing your own worst day, here's what I'll tell you: always listen to your inner self. Trust your gut. Stay prayed up. Stay humble. Stay consistent. Some things will go right; some things will go wrong. But even on your worst day, if you keep your faith and keep showing up, you'll always end up a winner.

Freddy Williams

From Coffin to Cocoon

My day came when a gavel fell and a sentence was spoken that seemed to be an attempt to silence my future. In that moment, the weight of the years pronounced pressed so heavily on me that I felt my knees buckle. Thirty-eight years. I would ultimately serve almost sixteen of those years.

I came to see that what was intended to be a coffin was, in truth, a cocoon. There's a vast difference between being buried and being planted. What they meant for evil, God made for my good. That dark day shaped me. It humbled me, stripped away pride, strengthened my faith, and ushered me into a season of purpose and growth.

Not *what* but *Who* helped me endure — primarily the Lord God. I would be remiss not to declare that God directed my steps and granted me favor. He protected, provided, and promoted. Above all, He renewed my mind, transforming me. Along with the grounding power of prayer, the unwavering love of my wife — who was my lighthouse — and my family, plus a deep conviction that this would not be the end of my story, I was sustained. Through that fire, the crucible of incarceration, I not only survived but thrived and was transformed.

If you are facing your own trying day, hear this: do not confuse a chapter with the conclusion, and don't ever allow a moment to stop a movement. In the scheme of things, everything is a moment — some longer than others, but all momentary, ephemeral. It will pass. It's incumbent upon us to stay in position and stay the course. The darkest night always yields to dawn. As Winston Churchill wisely said, "If you're going through hell, keep going."

Your pain has a purpose when properly viewed. Remember, where there is no struggle, there's no strength. Things aren't happening *to* you but *for* you — for your growth, your development, and your advancement. And in time, you will discover that what threatened to break you has actually built you.

Wayne Williams
Grow Through the Pain

One of the worst moments I ever had was when I fell asleep behind the wheel and got arrested for a DUI. I'd had a few chances before to get my act together, but I kept pushing my luck — until that day when it finally ran out. The whole process set me back, but it also woke me up. Sitting in that cell, I realized I had to make a change for the better. That experience forced me to confront my habits and take responsibility for my choices. I finally built up the strength to cut back tremendously on drinking alcohol, and that decision made a major difference in my mental health as well.

REFLECTIONS

What helped me push through was becoming part of the Financial Services Industry. I always tell people your environment is key. It's easier to remove escapism when you fill your life with positive distractions and purpose-driven work. Being surrounded by people focused on growth and success helped me rebuild my confidence and discipline. If someone reading this is facing their own "worst day," I would tell them this: **Don't just go through the pain — grow through the pain.** Personal development is key. You're already going through it, so you might as well get a reward for it. Use your struggles as stepping stones. The same moment that breaks you down can be the one that builds you up — if you decide to grow.

Chilly-O
The Last Fucking Party

One of my worst days didn't look like a breakdown. It looked like a party.

It was the "closing celebration" for Chilly-O Culture — the brand I built, the dream that I had for so long and then this happened, I walked around the side of the New Era building — out of sight, where no one could see — and I cried.

I let it fucking out.

Every ounce of disappointment. Every failure. Every unspoken fear.

I cried into the bricks, alone, because I couldn't let anyone see the leader fall apart.

That's when Tuki Carter, one of my closest brothers, ran up on me like a drill sergeant. Without hesitation, he grabbed me by the shoulders and barked, "Chilly-O, stop fucking crying! You are STRONG. Get your shit together!"

He didn't let me wallow. He pulled me back up in a way only Tuki can. And in that moment, I realized he was right — I couldn't let the tears drown me. I had to keep going, no matter how much it hurt.

That was only the second time I've cried as an adult. First time was my divorce. This one cut just as deep.

Failure Hit Different

That night, I felt like the biggest fucking failure in the world.

I felt like I let everybody down — the ones who believed in me, the ones who invested in me, the ones who championed the vision when it was still just an idea in my sketchbook. All of it felt like it went up in smoke.

But failure taught me something I couldn't have learned from success — real goddamn tenacity. Strength that doesn't come with applause. The kind of strength that shows up after the music stops and nobody's watching.

The crazy thing? I wanted to quit... but the people wouldn't let me. My community — the ones who rode with me — they kept showing up. Kept saying my name. Kept pushing me forward when I had nothing left.

Slowly, brick by brick, I built my confidence back.
But it wasn't about rebuilding the brand.

REFLECTIONS

It was about rebuilding me.
BMX Mentality, Fuck the Fear

I'm a BMX rider. I've fallen from 16 fucking feet in the air. I've landed on my back, my neck, had bike parts stab through my leg so deep you could see muscle. I know pain. I've danced with it. And I survived.

So I reminded myself: You've hit rock bottom before. You've bled and bounced back. Money comes and goes. Success fades. But grit? Grit's forever.

That night of the fight, I remember Blair Maxberry pulled me aside and said something that stuck in my soul:

"You can't control everything. If you're doing the work, sometimes you just have to believe — in the Universe, in God, in the infinite fucking energy of it all."

That was the moment. The pivot.

I realized I'd been trying to force life to obey. I was gripping too tight. And the harder I squeezed, the faster it slipped. I needed to let go — not in defeat — but in surrender. In trust.

Replace the Bullshit, Do the Work
So I made a choice. One fucking step at a time:
Remove the negative thoughts.
Not ignore them — replace them.
With intention. With purpose. With work.
Because the work? That's the real alchemy.

EVEN ON MY WORST DAY

I started waking up every day and asking: Who do I want to be today?

Not, What should I post? Not, How do I get the brand back?

But real shit: Am I aligned? Am I honest? Am I doing something that fucking matters?

The work became sacred. It was my therapy, my worship, my rebellion against everything that told me I was done.

It wasn't about success anymore. It was about service.
About showing up.
About healing out loud.

That night, I thought it was over.
But it wasn't the end. It was just the goddamn bottom.
And the bottom is a good place to build from — because there's nowhere left to fall.

When you survive a night like that — not just physically, but emotionally — you earn a kind of freedom most people never touch.

You learn that pain isn't the enemy.

Quitting is.

And I'm not a quitter.

Not now.

Not fucking ever.

REFLECTIONS

Klass Money
Things Always Get Better

One of my worst-day moments came when I made a bad investment deal in real estate and lost over fifty thousand dollars. It was one of those moments that shakes your confidence — when you start questioning your decisions, your judgment, and even your direction.

That experience taught me that everything is temporary. You have to be careful about what and who you invest in. But it also taught me patience — that in due time, everything gets better. Sometimes you just have to let go and let God.

What helped me push through was realizing that nothing fixes itself and no one is coming to save you. You have to wake up every day and work toward making things better. That mindset — that determination to keep moving forward — is what helped me overcome the loss and rebuild.

If you're facing your own "worst day," remember this: **things always get better.** No matter what it looks like right now, hold on to your faith and keep doing the work. God is good, and time has a way of turning pain into progress.

Robert Hayes
More Life. More Love. More I Am.

That day, my mom flatlined twice. The doctors resuscitated her both times. Telling them *not* to resuscitate her after she flatlined a third time was the hardest decision I have ever had to make — and the most abysmal directive I have ever given.

What made it worse was knowing that I was the one who persuaded her to go to the hospital against her will and better judgment. That conversation is vividly etched in my mind. She said to me, *"This is a minor issue, and I don't want to go! These white doctors don't care about Black people. They tell you your situation is more serious than it is, convince you to have an operation, then they chop you up and you end up dead."* I told her she was exaggerating. Seven days later, her words came to pass — and I was a 29-year-old son pulling the plug on his 55-year-old mother, a woman who had been relatively healthy.

That experience shaped me in ways I'm still uncovering. It made me a better listener, a more analytical thinker, and a more careful leader. I learned the power of influence — that I, and sometimes others, would have to live or die by the decisions I make. Since then, I've learned to respect all positions, analyze every piece of data, and make decisions more circumspectly.

It also birthed in me a passion to be a spokesperson and advocate for people who cannot speak for themselves or fight for their own rights. I sued that hospital for medical malpractice and walked away with a seven-figure settlement — because even on my worst day, my *status is plus*.

What helped me push through was my belief that God had me on a path destined to manifest His glory. Greatness requires sacrifice. Just as Abraham was willing to sacrifice Isaac, and God sacrificed His only begotten Son, I consoled myself by believing that my mother's sacrifice was part of God's divine plan — a necessary step in shaping my purpose.

REFLECTIONS

Christ in me, the hope of glory has been my mantra, my vision, and the driving force pushing me through both the best and worst of days.

If you're facing your own "worst day," hear me clearly: whether you are poor and lonely, rich and famous, or somewhere in between, find something greater than your everyday life to aspire to. Always keep a vision of *more* before you. Find something compelling that pushes and pulls you forward daily — this is how you keep from getting stuck, even on your worst day.

I believe God gives everyone a vision and a thirst for more — that's what faith is for. Discover that compelling vision and nurture it. Feed it with the right resources: books, movies, music, scripture, education, or like-minded people who share your desire to grow.

To me, *more* is the "plus" in Status Plus — **More Life. More Love. More I Am.** Always strive for more, and your status will always be plus.

Shawn West
Reawaken and Seize the Day

One of my worst-day moments came when my father passed away—and on that same day, while I was just trying to endure the pain, I got locked up and found myself sitting in jail. The shock and grief collided all at once, leaving me overwhelmed and broken.

That experience reshaped my outlook on life. It reinforced my understanding that you have to look within to create your own positive environment. You also have to allow those who are truly in your corner—

those who have your back—access to help amplify what already echoes in your heart.

What helped me push through was the time alone—the solitude that forced me to feel the full weight of the Lord's plan. There was no escape, only space to process the range of my emotions and let God do His work in me.

If you're facing your own "worst day," remember this: **find healthy ways to channel your emotions and use that energy to build a better tomorrow.** Whether you're heartbroken, broken, or feeling like there's no way out—breathe. Center yourself. Be careful not to cause others pain in your time of pain. And understand that death, though natural, is also a signal to the living: a call to reawaken and seize the day, the love, and the life you've been given.

Shevon Nedd
Change Is the Law of Life

My worst day was when I got locked up on a gun charge, facing real time. Sitting in that cell, I knew deep down that jail wasn't for me — and I made the decision right then that I wasn't coming back. I had to switch up my hustle.

They always say time changes things, but I realized you have to change things yourself. Change doesn't happen by waiting; it happens by deciding.

Change is the law of life, and those who look only at the past or the present are certain to miss the future.

REFLECTIONS

Manny "Mad Dog"
Even on My Worst Day, God Got Me

The day my father passed — nine years ago — was one of my worst days. When he died, it felt like he took a piece of me with him. Without my hero, I felt lost.

In that moment, I knew I had to step up and become the patriarch of the family. I had to be strong for my mother, because now all we had was each other.

What helped me push through was my faith in God — knowing that even though my dad wasn't physically with us anymore, he was still here spiritually. His presence lives on in me, guiding me, reminding me of the man I'm supposed to be.

Even on my worst day, God's got me. He has never given me anything I can't handle.

ABOUT THE AUTHOR

Maurice Williams is a visionary entrepreneur, author, and creative force behind Status Plus Fashions. Known for his signature mantra— "Even on my worst day, my status is Plus"—Maurice has built an empire rooted in resilience, authenticity, and purpose. From the streets of New York to the grind of Atlanta to the heart of Miami, his journey is one of transformation, faith, and relentless hustle.

Through his clothing line and now his book, Even on My Worst Day, Maurice shares raw lessons about life, love, loss, and leadership. His mission is to remind people that true status isn't about money or fame—it's about mindset.

Even on My Worst Day written and inspired by the life and entrepreneurial journey of Maurice Williams inspires readers to rise above their struggles, embrace their story, and remember that true strength isn't about never falling—it's about mindset. @statusplusfashions

www.ingramcontent.com/pod-product-compliance
Lightning Source LLC
Chambersburg PA
CBHW052053220426
43663CB00012B/2549